MW00638341

The Buddha Journey

Questions and Answers for the Awakening Mind

QUANG TRÍ

Published by Waldorf Publishing
2140 Hall Johnson Road
#102-345
Grapevine, Texas 76051
www.WaldorfPublishing.com

The Buddha Journey:
Questions and Answers for the Awakening Mind

ISBN: 978-1-944781-70-5
Library of Congress Control Number: 2016930008

Dedication

This book is proudly dedicated to my parents, J & A, and my sisters S, S & L.

My Dharma teacher, Ven. Thich Phước Quang.

My Sangha friends and family at Chùa Phước Huệ.

Finally, my person, B.J.L.

Namo Shakyamuni Buddha
Namo Shakyamuni Buddha
Namo Shakyamuni Buddha

Contents

Welcome

Welcome, Brothers and Sisters. Nothing helps us learn and grow better than asking questions. Even the most mundane questions can help us, no matter how basic or random it may be. Sometimes helpful information is hard to come by because there are so many different interpretations of the Buddha's teachings, so it might become confusing. This book, its teachings of history and methods, is as close and true to the original teachings as possible. Because we learn by asking questions, this question-and-answer format book will hopefully be very beneficial for you.

This book will cover several topics from the basics and history of Buddhism to meditation and contemplation, to cultivating loving-kindness and dealing with difficulty, and much more. *The Buddha Journey: Questions and Answers for the Awakening Mind* aims to help those that are beginning, interested in or advancing their Buddhist practice would ask in one simple book.

Smile and be well!
Quang Trí

Part I

History

Siddartha

The Buddha wasn't always the Buddha. Before his
enlightenment, Sakyamuni Buddha was Prince Siddartha
Gautama. Born on the night of the full moon in May
around 623 B.C., his mother, Queen Mahā Māyā, gave
birth to him in the Lumbini Park at Kapilavatthu.
Siddartha's father, King Suddhodana of the Sākya clan,
was eager to raise his son as a royal prince so he would
one day rule the kingdom.

Joyous about Siddartha's birth, an ascetic of high
spiritual attainments named Asita (also known as,
Kāladevala) visited the palace to see the royal baby. The
sage was asked to predict the child's future. The sage
replied to the king telling him that his son would either
grow up to become a great king and rule the kingdoms or
become a great holy man.

Queen Mahā Māyā, unfortunately, died seven days
after Siddartha's birth. Siddartha's aunt, Mahā Pajāpati
Gotami, who was also married to the king, adopted the

1

child and entrusted her own son, Nanda, to look out for young Siddartha.

Worried that Siddartha would leave the royal life one day, the king sheltered him inside the palaces and gave him every imaginable luxury. The king created an artificial environment so that everything was perfect and possible, and free of worries and suffering. The king never wanted his son to see that anything was wrong with the world so that he would continue staying in the palace and grow to become the next ruler. The king hoped Siddartha would not go out into the world and become a holy man as was predicted by the sage.

When the prince was 16 years old, his father married him to his cousin, Yaśodhara. For 29 years Siddartha enjoyed the palace life, never leaving, never seeing the outside world. The king constantly sheltered him and never let him outside the walls of the palace. Until one day, Siddartha finally made his way outside with his attendant for the first time.

Outside of his life of luxury and pleasure, Siddartha sees his first of four encounters. He sees an old man. Troubled, he asked his attendant why that man looked like that. The attendant replied, "That's change. One does not always stay young."

On his second visit outside, his second encounter Siddartha saw a sick man and asked his attendant what was wrong with him. The attendant replied, "That's sickness. It happens to all of us."

Siddartha's third encounter outside, he sees a corpse. Asking his attendant, the attendant replies, "That's death. We will all eventually die." Upon seeing the corpse, Siddartha realizes impermanence, suffering and death as the reality from his sheltered and luxurious life. Siddartha thought to himself, "This is my fate; to become old, sick, and die. How do I deal with these things?[1]"

On Siddartha's fourth encounter, he see's an ascetic[2] trying to overcome suffering, old age, sickness, and death. Troubled, Siddartha wanted to comprehend the nature of suffering and decided he wanted to leave the palace and go on a spiritual journey to answer his question.

Siddartha's wife had just given birth to a baby boy, Rahula, which means "fetter." On a late summer night, Siddartha entered his room where his wife and newborn son were sleeping. This was his goodbye. He then went to the courtyard where his horse was waiting for him and fled the palace, leaving his wife, his newborn child, father, and empire behind. Siddartha realized that in order to gain anything, one must lose everything.

---

[1] *The Buddha*. 2010. DVD. Directed by David Grubin. PBS Distribution.

[2] A person who practices severe self-discipline and abstention from all forms of indulgence.

For the first time, Siddartha was alone in the world. At a nearby river, he met an ascetic. He drew his sword and cut off his hair, traded his royal robes for the yellow robe of the ascetic and became homeless. Traveling South on the Ganges River, a prince that once had everything now had nothing. From prince to beggar, Siddartha traveled through the woods, slept on the cold ground, and begged for any scraps of food.

Siddartha didn't have any understanding, teaching, or insight yet. He recognized the problem but didn't have a solution yet. He couldn't get any help from the ancient Vedic religion at the time, a religion of ceremony and ritual. So he joined thousands of searchers, who like him, become renouncements to the world, embracing celibacy and poverty.

At the time, renouncements were a flourishing culture. Many wanted to find a way to escape the cycle of death and rebirth. The only way out was to become enlightened, to become a Buddha.

During his search for the truth, Siddartha came across his first teacher, a highly recognized guru who taught rigorous forms of yoga and meditation, and methods to tame the mind, desires and passions. Mastering all the methods and techniques of the guru, Siddartha ascended himself to these high levels of consciousness. However he knew it was impermanent, and it didn't penetrate the truth of the nature of reality, it

4

was only a temporary escape from the problems, but it didn't solve them.

Siddartha set out and met another accomplished guru, but the results were the same. He then thought to himself, "This practice does not lead to direct knowledge or deeper awareness," so he left his guru. He continued his search for the answers to his questions.

Asceticism was a common practice among the renouncements, punishing the body in order to attain wisdom and serenity. He subjected his body to extreme pain and hardships, doing everything he could to find his answers. Because the body was the common element of age, sickness and death, ascetics believed by punishing the body of these elements, they would be able to escape them. Siddartha met five ascetics, whom later on would become his first disciples.

For six years, Siddartha starved and punished himself in an attempt to rid himself of everything he saw as "bad," of everything that he sees as against the way of gaining his answers. Siddartha became extremely anorexic, he ate only one grain of rice a day, drank his own urine, stood on one foot, and slept on nails - he did everything to the extreme.

Siddartha's body was slowly withering away. In one of his stories, the Buddha said, "My limbs became like the jointed segments of vine. My spine stood out like a string of beads. My ribs jutted out like the jutting rafters of an old abandoned building. The gleam of my eyes appeared to be sunk deep in my eye sockets like a gleam of water deep in a well. My scalp shriveled and withered like a green bitter gourd. Shriveled and withered in the heat and wind."

Siddartha tried to push his body to the extreme as much as he could, but then he realized he wasn't gaining what he wanted. He was on the verge of dying when he remembered something; a day when he was young, and his father took him to a spring ploughing festival. Siddartha sat by the river and watched the ceremonial dancing. He looked down at the grass and thought about the insects and their eggs destroyed as the field was planted, he was very saddened. His mind soon started drifting. As if by instinct, he crossed his legs into the lotus position and the natural world paid him homage. As he sat there, he felt a sense of pure joy in the world that was already broken, in this transitory world we're all in.

Once Siddartha made this remarkable realization, he knew asceticism was not the way and that he needed to regain his strength if he wanted to continue his search. At that moment, a village maiden came up to him and offered him a bowl of rice porridge. Siddartha had failed. He had been clinging to asceticism and still hasn't found his answer, but he knew the extreme of luxury and the extreme of asceticism were not the ways. The five ascetics who were practicing with Siddartha saw him eating, upon this sight, they said, "Siddartha loves luxury. He has forsaken his spiritual practice. He has become extravagant."[3] So they left Siddartha alone in disgust and disappointment.

Siddartha had put his faith in two gurus and put his body into extremes, neither had given him the answers he was seeking. Now he knew what to do. To find the answer to his questions, he would look within and trust himself.

The Buddha

After accepting the bowl of rice porridge, Siddartha took off his robes, bathed in the river, sat down under the shade of the Bodhi tree and meditated. During a full moon in the spring, before the sun would rise, Siddartha's long search would be over.

As Siddartha sat under the Bodhi tree, he vowed not to get up until he gained enlightenment. Throughout the night, he meditated, and all his former lives passed before him. He gained the power to see life, death, and rebirth that all beings go through. As the morning star appeared, Siddartha said, "My mind is at peace." He had become the Buddha.[3]

---

[3] *The Buddha*. 2010. DVD. Directed by David Grubin. PBS Distribution.

The Buddha had realized that Nirvana, Enlightenment, was always there, is a part of everyone, but that our ignorance, greed and anger keep us from seeing it. All we have to do is eradicate our ignorance to be in Nirvana; that is the whole world around us. Nirvana is not a place or a destination; it is not something we can try to travel to and go to in the afterlife. Nirvana is here in the now; it is the quality of this moment.

For the next forty-nine days, the Buddha remained under the Bodhi tree enjoying the peace and joy of his realization. The Buddha contemplated whether or not he should teach the Dharma of his realization to others. He was concerned that people would not understand or believe him because they were so overpowered by ignorance, greed and anger that they would not be able to realize the path that is subtle, deep and hard to grasp.

Out of his great compassion, the Buddha traveled to the Deer Park in Sarnath[4] where he met the five ascetics he used to practice with. Seeing the Buddha walking towards them, they didn't want to welcome him and felt uneasy, but as the Buddha got closer, the ascetics saw how radiant the Buddha was, and they could not resist welcoming him. After offering the Buddha water to drink, the Buddha explained to them that he had found

---

[4] Saranath is a city located northeast of Varanasi in India. It is where the Buddha first taught the Dharma.

the path to enlightenment. The five ascetics then became his first disciples, and the Buddha taught them the Four Noble Truths (Dhammacakkappavattana Sutta). This discourse is referred to as *Setting in Motion the Wheel of Dharma.*

The Buddha did not preach a dogma. Instead, he spoke from his own experiences and hardships. He told his disciples that he had found a new way. Not a way of extreme luxury, nor a way of extreme asceticism, but a Middle Way. Like a string on a guitar that's too tight will break and the music dies. If the string is too slack, then there's no sound and the music dies. The Middle Way, tuning the string not too tight and not too slack, and there will be music for all to enjoy. The Buddha taught that the path to enlightenment lived in the Middle Way.

Finally, the Buddha was able to answer the question he'd been tirelessly trying to find. The answer was the Four Noble Truths. Buddha realized that suffering, or better translated as "dissatisfaction," is not something we can just get rid of. Instead, suffering is something we need to acknowledge and accept rather than try to push away and deny. Buddha discovered and taught us that life is unsatisfactory because there are causes; these causes are caused by our own mind. When we have wants and needs that are unattainable, we become dissatisfied and unhappy. These feelings of desire, greed, and anger are the causes we create for our own suffering.[5]

Buddha's first Noble Truth is that life is suffering, life is dissatisfying. The second Noble Truth tells us that our suffering has a cause; our wants, needs, desires, etc. The Third Truth is an important Truth; it tells us that we can be free of suffering if we can understand the cause of suffering. Buddha taught us that the problem is desire. However, there is good desire, and there is bad desire. We all desire to be enlightened, but is that desire also part of the desire we need to eradicate? No. We can have desires, but we must be smart about them. We need desire to live our lives. Without desire, where will we get the motivation to succeed in school or work in order to have a successful future? Without desire how will we accomplish important tasks or projects? Therefore, without desire, we cannot attain Buddhahood. Without the desire to become a Buddha, we will never accomplish our goal. Desires of greed, to harm, to lie and steal, to cheat – these are the desires we cannot have.

The Fourth and final Truth, the Buddha gave us our instructions manual, the guide to lead a life towards enlightenment; the Noble Eightfold Path – the cultivation of mindfulness, moral discipline, and wisdom.

---

[5] Schumann, Hans Wolfgang. 1989, 33-35. *The Historical Buddha: the times, life, and teachings of the founder of Buddhism*. London: Arkana.

After the Buddha explained the Four Noble Truths to the five ascetics, all five became Arhats.[6] It didn't take long before people started hearing about a great sage. The Buddha's disciples quickly swelled from a few hundred to a few thousand.

For the next 45 years, the Buddha taught the Dharma to a diverse range of people with different intellects and capabilities, using similes and parables in order to have everyone understand his teachings correctly in their own way.

Mahaparinirvana

In the *Mahaparinibbana Sutta*, the Buddha at the age of 80 announced that he would soon be reaching Parinirvana,[7] the final deathless state. The Buddha ate his final meal, which was an offering from a blacksmith named Cunda. Soon after, the Buddha became very ill and instructed his attendant Ananda to convince Cunda that his meal offering had nothing to do with his passing and that his meal would be a source of great merit as it provided the last meal for a Buddha.

---

[6] Arhat: an enlightened being who has attained Nirvana.

[7] The death of a person who has attained nirvana in their lifetime.

The Buddha asked his attendant Ananda to prepare a bed for him before two Sal trees, with his head facing north. Ananda, who served the Buddha for over 20 years, was deeply upset. "Don't grieve, Ananda!" said the Buddha. "The nature of things dictates that we must leave those dear to us. Everything born contains its own cessation. I too, Ananda, am grown old and full of years. My journey is drawing to its close, and just as a worn-out cart can only with much additional care be made to move along, so too the body of the Buddha can only be kept going with much additional care.[8]"

The Buddha asked his disciples three times if anyone had any doubts about his teachings or the disciplines. The disciples stood silent. "Not one, Ananda, has misgivings. All will eventually reach enlightenment." The Buddha then said his final words: "Listen, Bhikkhus[9], all conditioned things are subject to decay. Strive with diligence for your liberation."

Before Buddha's passing, his disciples asked him, "Teacher, please don't go. Who will be our teacher and teach us?" The Buddha replied, "Your precepts and Dharma will be your teacher."

Resting on his right side, the Buddha passed into

---

[8] The Mahaparinirvana Sutra.

[9] Literally meaning "beggar," a monk.

Mahaparinirvana.[10] For the next six days, the Buddha's body was honored with perfumes and garlands. On the seventh day, the body was taken to Mukutbandhana Chaitya,[11] the sacred shrine of the Mallas. During the cremation, the last ceremony was performed by Mahakasyapa.[12] After the cremation was completed, the ashes were collected by the Mallas as relics which included a skull bone, teeth, and inner and outer shrouds. These relics are enshrined in stupas[13] across Asia.

---

[10] The death of the Buddha.

[11] "Kusinara - Place of the Great Passing Away." BuddhaNet - Worldwide Buddhist Information and Education Network. http://www.buddhanet.net/e-learning/buddhistworld/kusinaga.htm.

[12] One of the principle disciples of the Buddha. He was foremost in ascetic practices.

[13] Stupa literally means "heap." It is a structure containing the remains of Buddhist monks.

Part II

The Basics

What Is Buddhism?

"What is Buddhism?" is actually a difficult question to answer. Depending on who we ask, where they're from, what their school/tradition is, and the amount of knowledge and understanding they have, each person will probably have a different answer. A basic answer is this: Buddhism is a religion, a philosophy, a psychology, and a way of life. It is the practice of love; loving-kindness and loving compassion. It is the practice to live in peace and bliss. A more complex answer would be: Buddhism is a practice of psychology, of the mind. It is a mind-centered religion aimed at eradicating the three poisons (ignorance, greed, and anger) that cause us to suffer and live in this cyclic existence of death and rebirth.

The Buddha taught us that the main factor contributing to our suffering is desire. Desire is what causes us to want the things we can't obtain. The things that we can obtain, we always want more of it or want the newest things. These desires turn into greed, and when our greed isn't satisfied, we become angry. Our anger causes us to be ignorant towards the true nature of reality. So, Buddhism is the practice of spiritual development that leads to the insight into the true nature of reality. A practice to teach us how to escape suffering, eradicate our ignorance, greed, and anger, and ultimately to become enlightened.

Unlike most other religions that base their faith in a god or deity, Buddhism is not a faith-based religion towards a higher being for one's liberation or access to heaven or a better life. Instead, Buddhism takes a firm stand that the only way towards our liberation or a better life is faith in ourselves. There is no god or deity figure in Buddhism. Buddha was not a god or a mystical being. He was human; he cried, bled red, got sick, and died just like a human. The Buddha taught relying on gods was not useful for those seeking enlightenment. What makes him extraordinary is his realization to the path to escape our constant birth, death, and rebirth. The main focus in Buddhism is in the practice (self-inquiry and experimentation in the teachings) rather than belief and faith.

The best way to explain Buddhism to people is to show them. Not showing them statues or relics, but rather the observation people make of you over time. Because Buddhists are constantly practicing loving-kindness, compassion, and generosity, and never swaying towards anger, frustration, or impatience, this simple way of living is the essence of being a Buddhist and the best way to show people what Buddhism is.

The foundations of Buddhism is in the teachings of the Four Noble Truths, the Noble Eightfold Path, and the Twelve Links of Dependent Origination. These basic yet complex Dharmas can liberate us on a basic level and put us on a path of greater understanding. It is very important to truly have a strong grasp and understanding of what might seem like "Buddhism 101," but this information is the foundation of anything else we will learn.

The Four Noble Truths

The Four Noble Truths (*catvāri āryasatyāni*) is the central doctrine of Buddhism. The Four Truths explain the nature of suffering (dukkha), its causes, its cessation, and the path to its cessation. Our suffering, or unsatisfactoriness, has three main aspects: 1) physical and mental suffering of birth, aging, sickness, and death; 2) attachment to things that are constantly changing; and 3) the dissatisfaction of everything that is impermanent, transitory, and not meeting our expectations.

The **First Noble Truth** is that life is suffering (Dukkha). For non-Buddhists or those new to it might take a dramatic reaction to the word "suffering," because they might think of suffering in its literal sense of pain, gore, and torture, but suffering here means "dissatisfaction." One thing to remember is that our own mind causes it. So what is suffering? In the physical sense, suffering is physical pain, injury, sickness, old age, and of course death. Mentally, suffering is disappointment, jealousy, depression, sadness, fear, anger, frustration, etc. There are many degrees of suffering, but life in its totality is imperfect and incomplete. "But life isn't always suffering – there are moments of happiness and contentedness," we might say. That's exactly what these are—MOMENTS! They are imperfect, impermanent moments that will eventually fade away. The Buddha taught that unless we can gain insight into the truth of reality and what can give us happiness and what is unable to give us happiness, the experience of unsatisfactoriness will continue.

The **Second Noble Truth** is the cause, origin, roots, creation, or arising of suffering (Samudaya). The main cause of suffering is attachment and desire. It's the attachment to transient things, not only physical transient objects, but also objects of our perception. Ignorance is the lack of understanding of how our mind is attached to impermanent things. Other reasons for suffering are craving, as well as striving for fame or glory, and the pursuit of wealth and prestige. Because there is an attachment to these transient objects, their loss is inevitable, thus causing suffering. The three main causes of suffering are the *Three Poisons*: ignorance (avidya), greed/attachment (raga), and anger/aversion (dvesha).

The **Third Noble Truth** is the cessation of creating suffering by refraining from doing the things that make us suffer (Nirodha). Cessation is the spiritual goal in Buddhism. Once we have truly understood the causes of our suffering, we can then eradicate these causes and be free from suffering. The cessation of these sufferings can be attained through Nirodha: the unclinging to sensual craving and conceptual attachment. This means that suffering can be ended by extinguishing all forms of clinging and attachment.

The **Fourth Noble Truth** is the path that leads to refraining from doing the things that cause us to suffer – *The Noble Eightfold Path* (Marga). It is the path of the Middle Way between the two extremes of excessive sensual self-indulgence (hedonism) and excessive self-mortification (asceticism), and will lead to the end of Samsara (the cycle of rebirth). The Noble Eightfold Path is a practical guide, which when developed together, leads to the cessation of our suffering. The paths are not "stages" that we can move from one to another. Instead, they are dependent on one another to work as one complete path or way of living.

The Noble Eightfold Path

The Noble Eightfold Path (*āryāṣṭāṅgamārga*) described by the Buddha is the path that leads to the end of suffering. It is a practical guideline for ethical and mental development with the goal of freeing ourselves from the Three Poisons. The Eightfold Path is not a step-by-step practice, it is practiced holistically. To have a right view or perception of something, we must also have right thinking, right speech, and right action in order to have right livelihood, right effort, right mindfulness, and right concentration.

The Eightfold Path is grouped into three groups that will lead us to enlightenment: Morality/Ethical Conduct (Sila), Wisdom (Prajna), and Meditation/Concentration (Samadhi).

- Wisdom (Prajna) – Right View and Right Intention.
- Morality (Sila) – Right Speech, Right Action, and Right Livelihood.
- Concentration (Samadhi) – Right Effort, Right

Mindfulness, and Right Concentration.

1. Right View (*samyāg-drishṭi*)

Right View is the deep understanding to see things as they really are, to deeply understand the Four Noble Truths. Right View is first because we need Right View to see and understand everything before we think it, speak it, do it, and live by it. It is to understand how our reality, life, nature, and the world as they really are – to see these things as impermanent and imperfect. It begins with the intuitive insight that all beings are subject to suffering, and it ends with complete understanding of the true nature of all things. Right View is also the ability to distinguish wholesome roots from unwholesome roots (or seeds) deep within our consciousness.

If we are honest people, it is because the wholesome root or seed of honesty is in us. If we live in an environment where our seed is watered, we will become honest people. But if our seed of dishonesty is watered, we may deceive those we love and care about. We might feel bad or guilty about it, but if this seed of dishonesty is strong, we may do it anyway. Practicing mindfulness helps us identify all the seeds in our consciousness and water the ones that are the most wholesome.

2. Right Intention (thinking) (*samyāk samkalpa*)

Right Intention refers to the volitional aspect: the mental energy to control our actions. This is the commitment to ethical and mental self-improvement; ridding ourselves of whatever qualities we know to be wrong and immoral. If we train ourselves in Right Intention, our Right View will improve. Because thinking often leads to action, Right Intention is needed to take us down the path of Right Action.

Right Intention reflects the way things really are, but the practice of Right Intention/Thinking is not easy. Our mind is often thinking of one thing while our body is doing another. Our mind and body are often not unified. When we're driving, we might be singing along to a song or swearing at other drivers while almost completely forgetting that we're driving! Conscious breathing is an important practice. When we concentrate and become mindful of our breathing, we bring our mind and body back together and become unified again.

There are three types of right intentions:

1. The intention of renunciation which means resistance to the pull of desire.

2. The intention of good will, meaning resistance to feelings of anger and aversion.

3. The intention of harmlessness, meaning not to think or act cruelly, violently, or aggressively, and to develop compassion.

3.   Right Speech (*samyāg-vāc)*

In short, Right Speech is:

1. To abstain from false speech, especially not to tell deliberate lies and not to speak deceitfully.

2. To abstain from speaking with a forked tongue; saying one thing to one person and something else to another.

3. To abstain from harsh and slanderous speech.

4. To abstain from exaggerating or embellishing speech; to not dramatize unnecessarily, making things sound better, worse, or more extreme than they actually are.

4.   Right Action (*samyāk-karmanta)*

Right Action refers to doing wholesome, compassionate deeds. Right Action can also refer to the Five Precepts. The *Cunda Kammaraputta Sutta* states to:

1. To abstain from taking life (harming sentient beings and suicide).

2. To abstain from taking what is not given (stealing, robbery, fraud, dishonesty).

3. To abstain from sexual misconduct.

4. To abstain from lying.

5. To abstain from consuming intoxicants.

5. Right Livelihood (*samyāg-ājīva*)

Right livelihood means that one should earn one's living in a righteous way, and that wealth should be gained legally and peacefully. The Buddha mentions four specific activities that harm other beings and that one should avoid for this reason:

1. Dealing in weapons.

2. Dealing in living beings (including raising animals for slaughter as well as slave trade and prostitution).

3. Working in meat production and butchery.

4. Selling intoxicants and poisons, such as alcohol and drugs. Furthermore, any other occupation that would violate the principles of right speech and right action should be avoided.

6. Right Effort (Diligence) (*samyāg-vyāyāma*)

To some, Right Effort should be the First of the Eightfold Path because Right Effort is the individual's will to achieve wholesome ethics and deeds. It is the mental effort and energy in doing wholesome or unwholesome thoughts and deeds. It's the same energy that fuels desire, envy, violence, and aggression, but it's also the energy that fuels self-discipline, honesty, benevolence, and kindness. Right Effort has four types of endeavors:

1. Prevent the unwholesome seeds that have not yet arisen in oneself.

2. Letting go of the unwholesome seeds that have arisen in oneself.

3. Watering the wholesome seeds that have not yet arisen in oneself.

4. Maintaining the wholesome seeds that have already arisen in oneself.

7. Right Mindfulness (*samyāk-smriti*)

Right Mindfulness is the mental ability to see things as they are, with clear consciousness. Mindfulness exercises a powerful grounding function. It anchors the mind securely in the present, so it does not float away into the past and future with their memories, regrets, fears, and hopes. Right mindfulness is cultivated through a practice called the "Four Foundations of Mindfulness" *(cattaro satipatthana):* the body, feelings, mind, and mental objections.

8. Right Concentration (*samyāk-samādhi*)

Right Concentration is described as one-pointedness of mind, meaning a state where all mental faculties are unified and directed onto one particular object. Right Concentration for the purpose of the eightfold path means *wholesome concentration*, i.e. concentration on wholesome thoughts and actions. Samadhi in meditation can be developed through mindfulness of breathing (Anapanasati), through visual objects (Kasina), and/or through repetition of phrases (Mantra). For meditation, the meditating mind focuses on a selected object. It first directs itself onto it, then sustains concentration, and finally intensifies concentration step by step.

There are two types of concentration: active and selective. Inactive concentration, the mind abides on whatever is happening in the present moment, even as things come and go and change. Active concentration means concentration on whatever is going on in our mind; allowing the thoughts and images to come and go without clinging onto them or entertaining them.

Selective concentration is holding onto and concentrating on one object. While doing sitting or walking meditation, we might concentrate on an image or statue of the Buddha. We are aware of the noises of the cars outside, of the thunderstorm, or the dog barking, but we only acknowledge them and continue with our concentration on our object.

We don't concentrate on an object to escape our suffering. Instead, we concentrate on making ourselves deeply aware of the present moment. Samadhi means concentration. To practice Samadhi is to live deeply in every moment. To concentrate, we should be mindful, fully aware and present of what is going on. Mindfulness creates concentration, concentration creates wisdom, wisdom leads to insight, and insight leads to enlightenment.

The Twelve Links Of Dependent Origination

Dependent Origination (Pratityasamutpada) is one of the most important teachings of Buddhism; it teaches the origin of suffering (dukkha) to be ignorance (avidya). In Buddhism, Dependent Origination is the teaching of how things come to be, are, and cease to be. The Twelve Links show how Dependent Origination 'works,' that no beings or phenomena exist independently of other beings or phenomena.

Each link is the cause of the next link (effect). Though the links are numbered and are in order, the numbering could begin anywhere because each link connects to all the other links. The Buddha explained dependent origination very simply as: "This is because that is. This is not, because that is not. This comes to be because that comes to be. This ceases to be because that ceases to be."

In many sutras this example is given: "Three cut reeds can stand only by leaning on one another. If you take on away, the other two will fall."[14] For a table or chair to exist, we need wood, a carpenter, skillfulness, tools, and many other causes, and each of these causes needs other causes to be. The wood needs the sun, the ground, rain, etc. A carpenter needs their parents, food, air, etc. The tools need the tool maker, machines or other tools, supplies, etc. And each of those things, in turn, has to be brought about by other conditions. Looking deeply at the trees, the clouds, and the rain, we can see the table and chair. The one can be seen in everything, and everything can be seen in the one. One cause is not enough to create an effect. At the same time, a cause must be an effect, and every effect must also be the cause of something else.[15]

1. Ignorance (Avidya)

Ignorance in Buddhism generally means lack of understanding, usually referring to the Four Noble Truths. It is also ignorance of Anatman (No-Self), the Skandhas, and Karma.

---

[14] A metaphor of Indra's Net or interbeing.

[15] Thich Nhat Hanh. "The Twelve Links of Interdependent Co-Arising." In *The Heart of the Buddha's Teaching*. New York: Broadway Books, 1999. 221-222.

2.   Volitional Formation (Samskara)

The volitional action, impulse, or motivation that comes from ignorance and creates thoughts, words, and actions that sew the seeds of Karma. When we have a lack of understanding, anger can arise.

3.   Consciousness (Vijñãna)

Very generally, vijnana is what happens when one of the six faculties (eye, ear, nose, tongue, body, mind) reacts to or becomes aware of one of the six external phenomena (visible form, sound, smell, taste, touch, and perceptions). Because of the first link of ignorance, we perform an action (the second link), this action plants a seed in our mind. At some point, through conditioning, a certain experience will occur because of the seed that was planted, whether good or bad. The actions of our body, speech, and mind plants seeds, or makes imprints in our consciousness. Whether we are acting physically, verbally, or mentally, we are conditioning the mind. The karma that we engage in, in this life, makes sets of imprints in our ongoing consciousness and these imprints eventually become the body we will have in the next life.

4.   Name and form (Nama-rupa)

Name and form is another term for the Five Skandhas (Aggregates). "Name" refers to the last four aggregates: feeling, perception, mental formations, and consciousness. "Form" refers to the first aggregate: form. As a collective idea, the Nāmarūpa motif models the reciprocal relationship of bodily and mental functioning. *Nāma* is the naming activity of the discursive mind. *Rūpa* develops an internal representation of external objects, without which mind and body cannot exist.

5.   Faculties and Objects/Six Sense Bases (Ṣaḍāyatana)

The Vijnana, or consciousness, link described above involves the six faculties or sense organs (ayatanas) (eye, ear, nose, tongue, body, mind) and six corresponding external phenomena, or objects (visible form, sound, smell, taste, touch, and perceptions). The faculties and their corresponding objects are the sadayatana. When a sense organ (sixth link) comes into contact with a sense object (fifth link), there has to be sense consciousness (third link).

6.   Contact (Sparśha)

Sparsha is contact with the environment, or the contact with the faculties and objects discussed of Sadayatana. When eyes and form, ears and sound, nose and smell, tongue and taste, body and touch, and mind and perceptions come into contact, sense consciousness is born.

7. Sensation/Feeling (Vedanā)

Vedana is the recognition and experience of sensations. These experiences are pleasant, unpleasant, or neutral, which can lead to attachment or aversion.

8. Craving (Tṛṣṇā)

There are these six forms of cravings: cravings with respect to forms, sounds, smells, tastes, touch, and ideas. If we are not mindful, we are perpetually being pushed around by desire for what we want and aversion of what we don't want. In this state, we heedlessly create karma, which keeps us entangled in the cycle of rebirth.

9. Clinging/Attachment (Upādāna)

Upadana is a grasping and clinging mind. We cling to sensual pleasures, mistaken views, external forms, material pleasure/comfort, routines, persons, and appearances. Most of all, we cling to ego and a sense of an individual self, a sense reinforced moment-to-moment by our cravings and aversions. We're attached to the objects of our desire and avoid the objects that are deemed unpleasant.

10. Becoming (Bhava)

Bhava is new becoming, set in motion by the other links. It means we are doing actual physical, verbal, or mental actions. The eighth link (craving) involved wanting or avoiding something, which leads to the ninth link (attachment), in which we made definite plans to get the object of our desire or to eliminate or avoid something that we have deemed unpleasant. In the tenth link, that decision is put into action. Good actions bring good results, and bad actions bring bad results. This link of becoming is of action, of creating karma. Because of that, we come to the eleventh link.

11. Birth (Jāti)

Jāti refers to the birth of a newborn being according to the specific karma created in the tenth link, in one of six realms (deva, asura, human, animal, hungry ghost, hell). Because of our karma, we will be reborn in samsara and experience life with all its pleasures and joys, pains and sufferings. We will go through various forms of suffering in life, because of our birth, which is dealt with in the twelfth link.

12. Aging and Death (Jarā-maraṇa)

Although aging and death are the two main forms of suffering for all of us, "Aging and Death" stands for all the various kinds of suffering, pains, and difficulties we will endure in life. All these are there because we have been born. Because we are born, we will age; because we are born, we will die. Thus, the inevitable cycle starts again until we have become enlightened.

Karma

We hear and read about karma all the time. Karma is a central aspect in Buddhist teaching because it's the energy that shapes our lives. To the commoner, karma is this invisible force that controls the fortune and misfortune of people. So if a driver cuts someone off on the highway, or broke into a car, it's the result of their bad karma. Karma works both ways; the person breaking into the car will accumulate bad karma, and the person that had their car broken into is paying back a karmic debt that they have.

Karma is a Sanskrit word meaning "action." In Buddhism, it's the principle of causality. Our thoughts, speech, and actions influence our present and future lives. Good deeds contribute to good karma and a good life, and bad deeds contribute to bad karma and suffering.

The nature of every action from the perspective of morality (every thought, every action, and every speech) can be classified in three ways: virtuous, non-virtuous, and neutral – or good, bad, and neither good nor bad. We've been accumulating karma for thousands or millions of lifetimes. It stays with us through our lifetimes in Samsara. It's because of the karma of our past lives that we have the life we have today; whether we were born into a rich or poor family, beautiful or ugly, smart or mentally challenged, or well built or disabled – it's all because of our past karma. The accumulation of our present karma will determine our future lives. If we've been doing virtuous things and accumulate good karma, we'll be reborn into a life of good circumstances and fortunes. But, if we're doing non-virtuous things, then we'll be reborn into a life of suffering and misfortunes, or even in another realm (hell, animal, or ghost realm).

There are six realms we can be reborn in Deva,[16] Asura,[17] human, animal, ghost, or hell. Only we can determine where we will be reborn based on the good or bad deeds we do. Every thought, speech, and action contributes to our karma and sows the seed in our consciousness. If we steal, commit sexual misconduct, or hurt/kill someone, those will affect our action karma. Slandering and lying affects our speech karma. Greed, anger, hatred, and ignorance affects our thought karma.

---

[16] Heavenly beings. Neither Devas nor Asuras are eternal and immortal.

[17] "Demi-gods" of the desire realm. Humans may be reborn in the Asura realm if in their lives they had good intentions, but committed bad actions.

As we sow the seeds of our thoughts, speech, or actions, we reap the results in the present life or in a future life. What we reap today is what we have sown in the present or past life. The *Samyutta Nikaya*[18] states:

"According to the seed that's sown,
So is the fruit you reap there from,
Doer of good will gather good,
Doer of evil, evil reaps,
Down is the seed and thou shalt taste
The fruit thereof."

Karma is essentially the law of moral causation.[19] Nothing is accidental or random; nothing is by chance when it comes to the circumstances of our lives. Everything has a cause and because of that cause it has an effect. Nothing happens to us unless it's something that we deserve, whether good or bad. We are simply either reaping the benefits of our good karma or paying back our karmic debt of bad karma.

---

[18] Samyutta Nikaya (Connested Discourses) is the third of the five nikayas (collections) in the Sutta Pitaka.

[19] Ven. Mahasi Sayadaw. "The Theory of Karma." BuddhaNet - Worldwide Buddhist Information and Education Network. http://www.buddhanet.net/e-learning/karma.

What is the cause of the inequality that exists among mankind?
Why should one person be brought up in the lap of luxury, endowed with fine mental, moral and physical qualities, and another in absolute poverty, steeped in misery?
Why should one person be a mental prodigy, and another an idiot?
Why should one person be born with saintly characteristics and another with criminal tendencies?
Why should some be linguistic, artistic, mathematically inclined, or musical from the very cradle?
Why should others be congenitally blind, deaf, or deformed?
Why should some be blessed, and others cursed from their births?

Karma is a law in itself that operates in its own field without any external entity or source. Asking where karma comes from is like asking where the wind comes from. It's not really important to know how or where it comes from, but that it's there, all around us, creating the path for our present and future life.

Our lives are governed by causes and effects. Ignorance and desire are the main causes of karma. Our happiness and sufferings are the inevitable effects of the causes. In Buddhism, these causes and effects aren't rewards and punishments assigned by a supreme, supernatural being to people who have done good or bad. Buddhism, which denies such supreme, supernatural being, believes in the natural law and justice of causality that cannot be created by a supreme, supernatural being or by a compassionate Buddha. This natural law bears the rewards and punishments according to the doers actions, whether human justice finds out or not.

Unlike other religions that state humans are born with sin or that our fate is sealed and cannot be changed, Buddhism disagrees and argues that regardless of how or where one is born, our circumstances can always be changed by our own efforts. If we are born in a poor, underdeveloped country or area, we can elevate ourselves and escape the area by studying hard in school, going to college, and getting a good job. College might not be free, but with the help of scholarships and grants, it can be of little cost. And almost everyone has access to financial aid, so being poor or living in a poor area is no excuse – you can change your future with your own efforts.

Classifications Of Karma

A) Karma can be classified into four kinds with respect to different functions:

1.   Reproductive Karma

Every life is conditioned by the past good or bad karma. Reproductive karma is the karma that conditions our future rebirth. When we die, we're simply going from one form of existence to another form. According to our potential thought-energy at the moment of death, i.e. our last thoughts, it is this final thought that is Reproductive Karma that will determine our existence in the next life, which could be good or bad.

2.   Supportive Karma

Supportive karma comes near and supports the reproductive karma. It assists in maintaining the actions of the reproductive karma during our lifetime and is neither good nor bad. If we are born with moral reproductive karma, supportive karma assists in giving us health, wealth, happiness, and good circumstances. If we are born with immoral reproductive karma, supportive karma assists in giving us hardship, sorrow, misfortune, etc.

3.   Obstructive/Counteractive Karma

Obstructive karma does the opposite of supportive karma. Instead of adding to the fortune or misfortune, it obstructs or interrupts the fruition of reproductive karma. If a person is born with good reproductive karma, they might be subject to various ailments or disabilities and unable to enjoy blissful results of their good actions. On the other hand, our pets are born with bad reproductive karma but lead comfortable lives eating good food, sleeping on a comfortable surface, and lounging around the house as a result of their good obstructive karma preventing the fruition of bad reproductive karma.

4. Destructive Karma

By the law of karma, the potential energy of reproductive karma could be voided by a powerful opposing karma of the past that is seeking the right opportunity to present itself. Destructive karma is more effective than supportive and obstructive karma because it destroys the whole force. Destructive karma can be good or bad.

The story of Devadatta is a great example of all four karmas. Devadatta attempted to kill the Buddha and caused a schism in the sangha. Because of his good reproductive karma, he was born into a royal family. His life of comfort and prosperity were due to his supportive karma. His obstructive karma came into place when he faced humiliation as a result of being excommunicated from the sangha. Finally, his destructive karma brought his life to a horrible end.

B) Karma can also be classified according to the priority of effect:

1. Serious/Weighty Karma

Serious karma may be good or bad. Its results are produced in this life or the very next life. If the karma is good, it is purely mental; Jhana (ecstasy or absorption), or verbally or bodily. If the karma is bad, there are five effective heinous crimes (*pancanantariya karma*): killing one's mother, killing one's father, killing of an arhat, wounding a Buddha, and creating a schism in the sangha.

If we were to develop the jhana and later were to commit one of the heinous crimes, our good karma would be eradicated by the powerful bad karma. Our subsequent birth would be conditioned by the bad karma, despite developing the jhana.

2. Proximate/Death-Proximate Karma

In most countries where Buddhism is practiced or in Buddhist cultures, the moments before death is extremely important by reminding the dying person of their good deeds and actions. Reminding the dying person of their good deeds while on their deathbed can aid in determining their future rebirth.

A bad person may die happily and have a good rebirth if they remember or do good deeds at the last moment. Likewise, a good person may die unhappily by remembering bad actions or unpleasant thoughts, causing them to have a bad rebirth. We might be reborn as a virtuous child to vicious parents, or as a vicious child to virtuous parents as a result of the last thoughts before death.

3. Habitual Karma

Habits, good or bad, become second nature to us, it creates our character as a person. During unmindful moments, we often lapse into our habitual mindset. So in the moment of death, unless influenced by other circumstances, we usually recall our own habitual deeds.

If it's in our habit to give our change to the homeless or to slander them, recalling this during the moments of death can alter our rebirth in a good or a bad life.

In the story of King Dutthagamini of Ceylon, he had the habit of giving alms to the monks before eating his own meals. It was this habitual karma that gave him joy during his moments of death, and he was reborn in Tusita heaven.

4. Cumulative Karma

Cumulative, or reserve karma are all the actions that are not included in the previous karma classifications and the actions that are soon forgotten.

C) Karma according to the time in which effects take place

1.   Immediately Effective Karma: karma that affects us in this present life.

2.   Subsequently Effective Karma: karma that affects us in the very next life.

3.   Indefinitely Effective Karma: karma that affects us in future lives after our subsequent life.

Meditation[20]

Contrary to popular belief, meditation isn't just about sitting crossed-legged, placing our hands on our knees with finger and thumb touching, and chanting "Om" repeatedly. It can be in a yoga class, but this isn't a yoga class. In Buddhism, meditation is many things: contemplation, awareness, insight, and finding inner peace and happiness.

Many resources, those new to meditation, and even the instructor in our yoga class will tell us to sit down, relax, and clear our mind. Unfortunately, it's not that simple. Clearing our mind is the end result, which may be many, many years down the road. If we ever even get there. Right now, meditation is about making friends with our mind. Meditation is about being mindful and aware of our mind and body, of its feelings, thoughts, and sensations in the present moment. It's about knowing

---

[20] From the author's book: *Making Friends With Our Mind: A Basic Guide to Buddhist Meditation.*

how the mind works in order to "override" it so we can handle whatever it throws at us.

Meditation is not passive; it's active. We don't just sit there, relax, and "clear our mind." What's the point in that? Meditation is about actively working on the mind, focusing it, eliminating distracting thoughts, and contemplating. The objective of meditation is to train the mind. By observing our mind, we can learn how it works, how thoughts and feelings arise, and how we acknowledge and handle them. For beginners of meditation, not being sucked into our thoughts is nearly impossible, but with practice and dedication, we can learn to be aware that we're being sucked in and slowly pull ourselves out.

Those new to meditation often try to find something through the experience, thinking that an "Aha!" moment will suddenly happen or that there's some finish line they need to cross. Meditation isn't a race, it isn't a destination, there's no expectations or finish lines. It's a never-ending practice. Meditation is simply being in the present moment and being aware of it. In the West, people want specific directions and techniques of meditation that will take them to this magical realm of peace and quiet. These techniques and magical places aren't important. What is important is the way of being present, mindful and aware of our body and mind right here and now.

In Buddhism, many books and teachers will say, "Take what I have just said and meditate on it." What exactly does that mean? In Zen, the Zen master gives a koan to his students, something as random as "What is a seashell that is neither a sea nor a shell?" The student then meditates and contemplates on this koan for as long as several years until he arrives at an answer that the Zen master accepts. When we contemplate in meditation, we take something apart, digest it, and analyze it until we see and understand every aspect of it. The first Truth in the Four Noble Truths, for example, is "Life is Suffering." What does this mean to us? What is life? Our life? People's lives? What is suffering and what constitutes as suffering? Suffering is translated from the Sanskrit word *Dukkha*, and it can sometimes come off as a very harsh or dramatic meaning. But what suffering really means is *dissatisfaction*. Dissatisfaction with life and all the good and bad things that come with it.

So when we contemplate on *Life is Suffering*, what we're really trying to do is realize that life is dissatisfying, that it is impermanent. Even the wealthiest of people are dissatisfied with their lives, whether it's because they want more money, or because all the money they have causes them stress and is too much responsibility. They become overwhelmed and depressed. Even for ordinary people, life is stressful, overwhelming, and depressing. We suffer because of our ignorance, greed, desire, and anger. So the point of meditating on suffering is realizing that we are ignorant because we don't know the Truth. We are greedy because we always want things for ourselves. We desire things we don't and can't have. And we become angry *because* of our ignorance, greed, and desire. When we contemplate these things, when we realize this is happening to us and then dig deeper into *why* we have ignorance, greed, desire, and anger, we learn the truth about ourselves. We come to a realization that, "Ah, maybe I'm always angry at my younger sister because I'm jealous of her success." These are the kinds of realizations we want to come to, because the more we know our minds and what causes us dissatisfaction, the better we can deal with them and avoid that kind of suffering in the future. When our mind is peaceful and free from worries, anxieties, and anger, we can experience true happiness. If we train our mind to become peaceful, we will be happy even during hectic and harsh conditions and circumstances.

Why We Meditate

Through meditation, we can do wonderful things. We can overcome our ignorance, delusions, greed, anger, hatred, jealousy, and depression, and enhance our compassion, loving-kindness, happiness, and equanimity. Meditation is the way we can find liberation to escape the bonds of dissatisfaction. A common problem that can come up during meditation is that we find this happy, magical place that gives us this sense of relaxation and peace – that's great and all, but it's important that we don't attach or cling to this feeling or special place. We must strive to push ourselves further and penetrate our mind deeper in order to escape the prison our mind has locked us in and find our way out to freedom.

Every being wants happiness. As humans we go from one thing to another in order to find that happiness; from one relationship to another, one job to another, or one city to another. We go to college and major in art, medicine, or creative writing in hopes that it will get us to a job that will make us happy. We adventure to new places to experience new foods and cultures, practice yoga, play video games, or grow flowers. Almost everything we do is an attempt to find happiness and avoid dissatisfaction. If we take a look at our lives, we'll discover that we spend a lot of our time and energy on mundane activities, such as seeking material, emotional, and sexual satisfaction, and enjoying the pleasures of the senses. Although these things can make us happy temporarily, they can't provide us lasting and true happiness. Eventually, all the pretty things we have, feelings we get, and pleasures we experience will end and become dissatisfying. We then find ourselves again and again going after these external pleasures and again eventually becoming dissatisfied. By becoming attached to worldly pleasures, it directly or indirectly causes us to suffer. Our desire to have the latest tech gadget gives us temporary happiness until the next new gadget comes out and we again desire to have it, and if we can't we suffer. Everything will end; everything is impermanent. Our house will eventually age and fall apart. Our car will also age and stop running. Our loved ones will age, get sick, and die. If all we're doing is trying to find external happiness in material or emotional experiences, our mind will never be at peace.

Happiness can come from external pleasures, but it doesn't truly satisfy us and free us from our problems. It is unsatisfying, transitory, and unreliable happiness. This doesn't mean we have to give up everything we enjoy like friends and possessions. Rather, we need to give up the misconceptions of what they can do for us. At the root of our problems is the fundamental mistaken view of reality, because we see these things as permanent and able to satisfy us "forever." We have an instinctive belief that people and things exist in and of themselves; that they have an inherent nature, an inherent thingness. This means we see things as having certain lasting qualities within them; that they are good or bad, attractive or unattractive. These qualities seem to be in the objects themselves as independent of our viewpoint and everything else.

For example, we think that ice cream is inherently delicious, or that having lots of clothes is inherently satisfying. If they were, surely they would never fail to satisfy or give pleasure, and we would all experience them in the same way. Our mistaken ideas are deeply programmed in our mind and are habitual to us; it controls our relationships and experiences with the world. We probably never question on whether or not the things we see is the way they actually exist, but once we do we'll be able to see that our view of reality is exaggerated and one-sided. That the things we see as good or bad, attractive or unattractive are the things we've created and project by our mind.

Happiness is a state of mind. Therefore, the real source of happiness lies within ourselves, not in external circumstances. Though there is nothing wrong with having possessions and enjoying pleasures, we, however, tend to cling to these things and when they end or disappear we suffer. If our mind is peaceful and free from attachment, greed, ignorance, and anger, then we will become happy. Likewise, if our mind is not peaceful and free, we will become unhappy. So the purpose of meditation is to cultivate these states of mind of peace and happiness and eradicate those that are not. The Buddha said that it's a great gift to be born as a human, because only as a human do we have the chance and ability to gain enlightenment. Animals can enjoy food and sex, build homes, and care for and protect their family, but they can't completely eliminate suffering and find true happiness. So why as humans do we sometimes only achieve what animals can do? As humans, we must use our precious time to study and practice virtuously so we can escape the cycle of Samsara. Meditation helps us break the mundane walls of our attachment, ignorance, and greed and lift us out of the prison of our mind to find love, happiness, and freedom.

When, Where, And How?

There is really no "best" time to meditate. Anytime is the best time to meditate. Meditation should be an all-day awareness practice; to be mindful of everything we think, say, and do. However, the easiest time to meditate is early in the morning, before we start our daily routine and chores. It's easier in the morning because our mind and body are fresh, and we haven't done much for the mind to wander off and think about. If we meditate in the evening or late at night, our minds are full of the memories, ideas, thoughts, and feelings of the day, so we'll be constantly going over these thoughts and feelings, and it'll distract us from our true meditation practice.

Where to meditate is just as important as when to meditate. This part is probably obvious because we already know it should be in a quiet place where distractions are minimal to none. That's true. Until we are meditation masters, noise and sounds will always be a distraction, no matter how soft or distant it may be. So until we can enter a state of meditation where we can block out all the outside world, it's important to find a peaceful and quiet place to be able to relax for a reasonable amount of time without being disturbed. Once we've found a spot, it's also important that the temperature is comfortable. Not too hot and not too cold, but just right!

Meditating outside in fall or winter weather is probably the best time to meditate. We've probably seen images or videos of monks meditating in the snowy Himalayas with ease. We can do the same. However, this is no easy task. The amount of energy and concentration these monks have is a lifetime of practice. Using the Nine Levels of Meditation as our guide (covered in Part VI), we can assess ourselves on where we are and where we need to be to develop full and perfect concentration. It takes a gifted meditator to reach any of the higher levels of meditation, but even reaching levels two and three is a major accomplishment. So practicing outside when it's slightly chilly or cold is great concentration practice.

Obviously, we may need to wear comfortable and protective clothing. We don't want to be freezing, but comfortable enough where we can feel the chill. When it's hot or cold, our skin senses it and sends messages to our brain letting it know, "Hey! It's cold/hot!" With continuous practice, we can learn how to yield or distract these messages, and we can then bypass the feeling that it's hot or cold. But once the concentration is broken, that sudden chill or heat will rise and slap us right in the face.

So how do we meditate like those gifted monks in the snow? Using focus points. Having an object of focus during meditation is extremely important in developing our concentration. Without an object to focus on, our minds will simply wander and become distracted with our thoughts. Using an object of concentration helps us to a) eliminate those distracting thoughts, and b) become mindful to go back to our object when the thoughts do manage to distract us. Objects of concentration are many. The most common and traditional is following our breath. Other objects that can be used are mantras, images, candlelight, the sound of a clock ticking, malas, or anything else we want to use and can concentrate on without being pulled into the object and become entertained by it. For example, if we use an image of our parents, focus on it without thinking, "I remember that day. We did this and that, and I was this many years old," etc. So it should be a simple image, maybe of the

Buddha, a Bodhisattva, or of a flower. Something simple. The sound of the clock ticking is a very effective object of meditation for beginners or intermediate meditators. Because it is constant and predictable, we can focus on the ticking sound in a few different ways. One way is to simply listen and concentrate on the sound, to a point where we are almost mesmerized by it, and all other sounds seem to melt away. This gives us a strong focus point with minimal distractions. Another way is to use the ticking to breathe. For every two or three seconds, we inhale and then exhale for another two or three seconds. Though this method is breaking the rule of "don't control the breath, just watch it," it serves a basic method of focus. Eventually, we'll forget to "control" the breath and just breathe normally but still keeping our concentration on the clock ticking.

The point of maintaining our concentration is to not allow distractions to actually distract us. Using mindfulness, when a sound is heard, for example, the doorbell or phone ringing, we don't want to go after it and wonder "Who's at the door" or "Who's calling me?" We simply want to acknowledge the sound, note it, and move on without sinking into the thought. There are good thoughts and bad thoughts. Bad thoughts are the thoughts that grab a hold of us and pull us into their trap of engaging with them. Good thoughts are the thoughts that arise from being in the present moment; by watching our breath, the rise and fall of our abdomen with that breath, or feeling the air going in and out of our nose as we breathe. Thoughts of contemplation are also good thoughts. Any thought that naturally allows us to gain insight and cultivate good qualities is considered a good thought. Any thought that makes us think of the emotions, feelings, and worries of the past or the anxieties of the future is considered a bad thought.

Part III

Compassion and Loving-Kindness

What Is Metta?

Mettã means loving-kindness. It's the unselfish act
of treating everyone with loving-kindness, friendliness,
kindness, and compassion. Mettã Bhavana is the
cultivation (or meditation) of loving-kindness. It's the
way for it to grow strong, powerful, and useful because it
brings us and everyone else deep and intense peace and
happiness.

Mettã is also the strong wish for the happiness of
others. For us, it also shows patience, appreciation,
compassion, and receptiveness. It shows the caring for
the well-being of all sentient beings. By practicing and
truly holding loving-kindness, others' happiness will also
bring us happiness and joy.

There are a few different methods to meditate on
Mettã. One of the more common ways is to think of
one's self; a loved one (family, friends), a neutral person
(the banker, cashier, stranger), a foe (or someone you
dislike or dislikes you), and finally towards all sentient

beings. While meditating on each person, we can say something like:

May I (s/he) be free from enmity/danger.
May I (s/he) be free from mental suffering.
May I (s/he) be free from physical suffering.
May I (s/he) take care of myself (her/himself) happily.

Or you can say the form from the *Cunda Kammaraputta Sutta*[21]:

May these beings be
free from animosity,
free from oppression,
free from trouble,
and may they look after
themselves with ease!

Regardless of what way or form we say it, do it! It's important to have loving-kindness. Not just for others, but for yourself as well. It helps us overcome anger, gives us concentration, and a healthy relationship with every sentient being.

---

[21] Cunda Kammaraputta Sutta (To Cunda the Silversmith, AN 10.176) translated from the Pali by Thanissaro Bhikkhu, 1997.

I deal with people on a daily basis, and at least 50% of them are rude, in a bad mood or just not up for the day. Back in the day, anyone that was rude to me, I was rude right back. My mouth was quicker than my thoughts! Sure, it got me in trouble sometimes, but at the time, I thought it was worth it. But what did that prove? What did me mouthing off at them do? Nothing for me, and surely just gave the person what they were probably after, attention and feeling noticed. What does loving-kindness do? It gives us mindfulness and concentration. It gives us the power to show patience and respect even in heated moments. It shows that their anger, hostility, and probably direct attempt to ruin our mood isn't even going to be noticed because of our radiant loving-kindness.

One time I was at a gas station getting gas after I was leaving temple. As I was filling up, this older man in an old beat up car slowly walked over and gave me this little story how he was just trying to get down the road to the hospital to see his mother and was wondering if I had two or three dollars to spare for gas. So I went over to his pump and swiped my card. "Four dollars?" he asked. I smiled and bowed my head in agreement. The man put in exactly four dollars. He thanked me, at least, a dozen times, and I simply just put my palms together and bowed.

Once he left, a man at the pump directly next to mine asked me why I gave him money. I was shocked as to why he asked or if that somehow bothered him. "He could have done anything with that money," he said. "Sir, I don't care what he does with the money. I used my card anyway. He only asked for four dollars, and he seemed sincere. Why should I say no if I don't have to?" I replied. He then said, "Well I guess if you have the money!" As I gave him a face, I replied, "Sir, by no means do I have ample amounts of money. If you were ever a college student, maybe you'd know how it feels never to have extra cash. But when someone's in need of something as simple as four dollars and if I'm able to give it, then I will."

Moral of the story: Loving-kindness can happen in many different ways. It's important to cultivate it, use it, and spread it to others. Even though the second man asked and argued with what I did, I'd hope I, at least, set an example. Saying and thinking about loving-kindness is easier than doing it. Loving-kindness isn't just something we can do for part of the day until someone really pisses us off or puts us in a bad mood. No! Use that to meditate on loving-kindness and release those negative feelings. Show others our compassion and understanding, and show them their negativity won't harm us or our karma!

How do I deal with difficult people?

In the mundane world, we deal with difficult people almost on a daily basis. Whether they're classmates, co-workers, bosses, neighbors, or random people – difficult people are everywhere! As Buddhists, we should know how to deal with such people and how to control ourselves. Yes, dealing with difficult people can be difficult, but just like our spiritual practice needs practice and development, so does our patience and compassion. Which just happens to be the solution to the problem!

With our patience and compassion, we can overcome and let go of people's negativity, rudeness, and ignorance. So maybe you're the boss's person that gets them their coffee every day. Your boss is rude and insensitive who never says please and thank you (which by the way, is part of loving-kindness practice, to not accept returns from acts of kindness!). You bring them their coffee every morning, and you stand there waiting for a thank you and get nothing. Not even a glance or a grunt to acknowledge that you're even there. So you walk away and sigh.

Don't. Instead, the next time you bring them their coffee, make that cup of coffee the best coffee you've ever made! Put love and effort into it, make it a coffee that is worth savoring each sip, a coffee they'll remember! Do this for a while. Then, take some cookies or a muffin with their coffee. Something you know they like or might enjoy. Do that for a while. Every time you take them their coffee, cookies or muffin, do it with a smile and tell them to "enjoy!" A smile is the best weapon for every attitude! Eventually, your boss will notice. Not only the really good coffee and treats, but they'll notice you and your attitude. Maybe they'll make eye contact, nod, grunt, or eventually even say thank you!

Your patience and compassion was noticeable! Yes, it might take some time sometimes, but it never fails. Often people treat rudeness with rudeness, and that's *never* the right thing to do. That will literally just make things worse. If someone is rude to you, who cares! Their attitude and ignorance doesn't affect you whatsoever. Only YOU can affect you! You simply treat their rudeness with a smile and a 'thank you.' Tell them to have a great day. Kill them with kindness! Sometimes this makes them even angrier and even more rude, but once they walk away and think about it, they'll think, "That person was really nice to me, and I took out my frustrations on them. Next time I'll be nice to them."

Some people's personalities are just rude and unkind, and maybe no amount of patience and compassion will affect them, and they'll just have to suffer and spend an even longer time in Samsara. But other people might just be having a bad, rough, long day, or they might be in a hurry, and they're just not in the

60

mood to talk or pay attention to you, so they're rude and unkind. So why would you want to make their day worse and be rude and unkind back? Instead, smile. Your smile will remind them to smile too, and it'll have some effect on their mood and make it just a little bit better.

The Buddha once told this story: An ugly, hideous, smelly, and gross looking monster went to see an emperor at his palace. When the monster walked in, the guards saw the monster and knew he didn't belong there, so the guards screamed at the monster, calling him names and threatening the monster. And for every rude thing the guards said, the monster grew one inch bigger, uglier, and smellier. The guards then pulled out their swords, waving and striking it towards the monster and still yelling at the monster, and with every strike and word, the monster grew one inch bigger, uglier, and smellier. The monster got so big that it took up half the size of the courtyard. Then the emperor walks in and sees the monster. The emperor opened his arms and yelled, "Welcome!" And the monster grew one inch smaller, less ugly and smellier. The emperor offered the monster water and food, and the monster grew smaller, less ugly and smellier. And with every kind word, gesture, and action, the smaller, less ugly and smellier the monster got. The monster got so small, that one more kind word it would disappear, and it did.

So remember this story. No matter how ugly (verbally) or unkind someone may seem, patience and compassion will seize the day! So always practice and strengthen your patience and compassion. Remember it can help you and the other person, and then that person will remember your patience and compassion and hopefully develop those skills for themselves and practice it. Show people how to act and be. The best way to be a Buddhist is to practice compassion and have others see that in you and practice it themselves.

I work at a fast-food place, and I find it hard to be compassionate when customers are being rude. What can I do, so that I can see these people in a better light and not be absorbed by my anger and hurt?

I want you to take their anger and serve it to me on a plate—with a side of rudeness. You can't! Because it's not really there. All feelings and emotions are only false perceptions of your mind; they are there because you allow it to be. If your mind doesn't have any anger, then anger externally doesn't exist!

The Three Poisons in Buddhism are ignorance, greed and anger, eradicating these poisons brings us to peace; to nirvana!

There's no way for you to make people not angry and rude; it's going to happen to anyone, anywhere no matter who you are or where you work. The solution is training your mind to see these as temporary, false feelings. Unless you're psychic, you probably have no idea what 99% of the people you interact with are going through. We are all human, which means we all have good days and bad days, and most people let their bad days become bad attitudes, and it affects the people around them. But you can be one of those people that it won't affect if you train yourself to simply accept the anger and negativity and let it pass. It can't affect you unless you allow it to.

This is not an easy overnight process. It will take time, lots of time. I'm still in training! But like the clouds in the sky that come and go with different shapes, sizes, and colors, so do emotions and feelings, so why cling to them?

Lately, I've been practicing to love myself and others around me. But it's so easy to hate.

Hate is actually very unnatural. We are not born to hate. We are born with the natural ability to love. The only reason we hate or discriminate is because society has shaped us that way. If you put a bunch of children together of different races and ethnicities, they're not going to segregate themselves into a group of white kids, a group of Asian kids, and a group of black kids. Instead, they're going to play and love each other. It's only when we grow older that society and the environment around us teaches us to segregate, discriminate, hate, and become ignorant.

It's easy to hate, but what is that hate doing for us? When we are angry, how long are we angry for? A few minutes, maybe an hour or a day, but then that anger goes away, and we might even forget why we were even angry in the first place. When we are happy, that happiness radiates from us like the first rays of sunshine rising from the mountains; it's big, noticeable, and affects everyone in the area.

The simplest thing we can do when a difficult situation arises is to just accept it and let it go. It's easy to get frustrated when someone cuts us off on the highway, but instead of wanting to be vengeful and speed up and cut them off too, we simply just accept that the situation happened, be grateful that an accident didn't occur, and continue to our destination. Because what's going to happen if we allowed that anger to take over? We're going to speed up, cut them off, and cause an accident. Now our car is totaled, we might end up in the hospital, or worse, dead. Is that worth the temporary anger that we'll forget about by the time we reach our destination?

Instead, acknowledge, accept, and let difficult situations come and go. Be a role model in difficult situations; show loving-kindness, patience, and compassion. When people see us smiling and see that the difficult situation doesn't affect us, maybe next time they'll do the same and realize anger isn't worth it.

When difficult situations arise, go back to our breath. Take deep breaths and concentrate on them. Don't think about the situation, don't think about what we could have said or done differently. Just listen and feel our breaths. Chant a mantra, out loud or in our head. Chant "Om Mani Padme Hum" and concentrate on the words. The longer our mind is off about the difficult situation, the quicker we can overcome it.

In order to find inner peace, to feel calm, I have been looking inside of myself. The problem is that when I do so, I do not like what I find. I have come to dislike myself quite deeply. I wish to understand how I can come to love myself once more when I hate who I am.

Ask yourself, "Who am I?" We usually describe ourselves by our name, gender, preferences, education, etc., that's what we think makes us *us*. But that's not true. Our *true self* is not of this body-mind phenomenon. Our body is simply a vessel, a hotel that we're checked in at during this life. This body is giving us the causes to discover who we really are, and everything that happens in our life are just obstacles distracting us from our path.

So what do we do in order to love ourselves again? What do we do to put ourselves back on the path to discovery? To help others, we must first help ourselves. To love others, we must first love ourselves. Know and understand that our past is simply that; history. We can't go back, we can't change it, we can't do anything about it, so instead of lingering over it and hating ourselves, just accept it and move on. What's benefiting you by hating yourself? By hating your past? You're doing a disservice to yourself and others. It's important to meditate and reflect on the core issues of *why* you dislike yourself. Maybe it's because you did or said bad things, but then go deeper and find out why you did or said those things, and why you would even have the thought to do or say them in the first place.

To find inner peace, we have to practice loving-kindness and loving-compassion on ourselves. Peace comes when we've let go of attachments, desire, greed, and ignorance. We may have become attached to our past faults, so that's blocking our path to peace, but we can break through that blockage by accepting those faults and penetrating them with love. In Buddhism, we don't have enemies, the only enemy is ourselves, so without conquering and freeing ourselves, there's no winning, no peace, no happiness, and no liberation. Don't define who you are by your past, there's nothing you can do about it. Define yourself by your awareness of the present moment, the ability to know you are the master of the moment and can change your future (and your future lives).

"You yourself, as much as anybody in the entire universe, deserve your love and affection." – Buddha.

And when you truly love yourself, you won't be able to hurt others. So meditate on yourself. Accept the past and let it go, don't attach to it. Then, live in the present moment. By being aware and mindful of your thoughts, speech, and actions, you can stop every ill intention.

Lately, I've been practicing to learn to love myself and others around me. But it's so easy to hate. Could you give me any advice on the subject?

It's habitual to hate people and things that annoy us, frustrate us, and cause us suffering (dissatisfaction). But we need to ask ourselves: Why? Why do these things bother us? It's so much easier to hate than to love. It's so easy to hate and curse at the driver that cuts us off. It's easy to hate the person walking in front of us who doesn't hold the door open for us. It's easy to get frustrated with our friends, siblings, and parents – but what is this doing for us? Absolutely nothing!

It's not easy to let things go and just pass, but that's exactly what we have to do. We have to just let the things happen and move on. Accept that someone cut us off, accept that the person didn't hold the door open for us, and accept that our friends, siblings, and family are driving us crazy. Accept what's happening, breathe, and just smile at them. Because once whatever has happened happens, there's nothing we can do about it. We can't go back in time and change it, so why suffer? Why hold on to that anger, to that hate, to that anxiety and frustration? What is it doing for us?

So what's the solution? Conditioning. We have to condition ourselves and our mind to just accept things and let it go, and smile. It's so easy to hate all we want on the driver who cut us off. We might even want to be vengeful and speed up and cut them off too! But what's that going to do? It's going to cause an accident. It's going to ruin our car. It might even put us in the hospital, or even worse, kill us. So is that worth our temporary vengeance to get back at them? Probably not, right? Instead, be a role model, be an ideal. Show them loving-kindness and compassion. We can laugh at the situations if we want to. Just smile and let it be. So when they see us smiling and see that what they did, did not affect us, maybe next time they'll think about what they did and won't do it again.

We have to condition our mind to think positive, to do positive, and to be positive. Always smile, even if we're just walking to our car or driving, waiting in line, or simply just sitting down. We attract what we put out. Everything is a cause and effect: we do good, good things will happen – we do bad, bad things will happen. It's a challenge to not just want to hate everyone, but if we practice daily loving-kindness meditation (or at least as often as we can), eventually even the rudest of people we can forgive and forget.

It's easy to hate, but it can be easier to love if we dedicate and really apply ourselves to be compassionate and spread loving-kindness to everyone. Throughout the day, we can chant the "Om Mani Padme Hum" mantra or any other mantra, so if a difficult situation arises, we can go back to the mantra and remind ourselves to be compassionate, to smile, to let it go. We don't want to affect or gain bad karma because of the angry thoughts that might arise, so if we just chant or hum a mantra, our mind will be concentrating on loving-kindness.

I'm just beginning to learn about Buddhism. My question is how to handle when someone

*deliberately disrespects you? How do you stay
enlightened, and what is the best way, spiritually,
going about the situation?*

The best way to go about the situation is to simply
let it go. I know it's easier said than done, but there's no
better way to deal with such people than to show
compassion to them. We want them to know that we
won't sink to their level of ignorance and hate.
Psychologically, when a person disrespects, is rude or
mean, etc., it's simply a defense mechanism because they
feel unworthy or superior. So by showing compassion,
we're stating that we are neither as low as they are or as
superior – we're simply the better person that can handle
the situation.

We want to lead by example. Perhaps if this person
is difficult several times and we're always doing nothing
but sharing loving-kindness and loving-compassion, then
maybe they'll finally walk away and say, "they're always
nice to me when I'm rude to them. Maybe next time I can
try to be a little nicer." Eventually, that will happen. It
might take time, but that will be the end result.

We want to let things go because we can't change
what already happened. We don't have a time machine to
go back and stop a person from doing or saying
something. So the best thing we can do is acknowledge
what happened, learn from it, and move on.

Just because someone insults us, doesn't make us what they call us. If someone calls us an idiot, does that actually make us an idiot? No, it doesn't. If someone else calls us ugly, does that physically make us ugly? No. We know we're not an idiot, so why believe it or let it affect us if someone says that? There's no point, right? People who complain, insult, or are just plain difficult are people who are probably neglected and simply want attention in any way, shape or form. And if we feed that attention with the same attitude they give (anger, hate, etc.), then we're just making it worse for the both of us.

The Buddha said, "Hatred never ceases by hatred, but love alone is healed." Live by that mantra and we and a lot of people we encounter will become much happier people.

How do you learn to let go of your past? (Especially an ex). I have read the book "The Power of Now" and have tried to meditate, but I find myself thinking of things that have no significance now at the moment. The past 6 months have been very difficult for me; I feel like I'm becoming emotionless because whether I try or not, I feel I get nowhere. I don't even remember the last time I felt real happiness. Everything is blah. Nothing

moves me. It's not a good feeling at all. Any advice on this?

This time last year we were probably mad, angry, or depressed about something – what was it? We probably can't remember, right? Because it doesn't matter anymore. That's the attitude we need to have in the Present. The Power of Now book is an amazing book and holds a lot of truth that should be practiced regularly. When someone is in an angry mood and perhaps yells at us, somehow their anger transfers to us, but then we should always try to ask and remind ourselves, "Why?" We ask "why" because how and why do people's attitudes and rudeness affect us? Why does it matter? What good is getting upset about it going to do for us? We become angry and moody because we allowed it. No one else caused us to get angry or moody but ourselves. If we were mindful, we would instead be aware of the emotions that rise, remind ourselves that they are not important or significant and let them go without causing any agitation to us.

We don't remember happiness? Ask ourselves another question, "What is happiness?" If to us happiness is someone (a significant other) or something (material objects), then we don't know what happiness is yet. True happiness comes from within. Any other happiness is only temporary – our significant other will age, get sick, and die; our car, house, new phone or computer will get old, fall apart, and finally deteriorate into the Earth. So why would that bring us happiness knowing that everything will not last? What will last is our true Self and our inner happiness!

This doesn't mean we can't love people and want material things because we can! But what we *can't* do is think that they'll give us lasting happiness. If we meditate on impermanence and recognize that everything is temporary, it makes things easier when they finally disappear or leave. We can't rely on people and things to make us happy. Only we have the ability to make us happy. It isn't easy, but we can at least try. Like everything else, it takes practice and patience.

The point is, the past is exactly just that – the past. There's absolutely nothing we can do about it now. So instead of regretting and depressing over the past and worrying about the future, we need to focus our energy on the present – the only time where things actually matter! The past might have hurt us, but only by focusing in the present can we be healed. By acknowledging and being mindful of our emotions we can better be aware of how we're feeling, and then take a look at those feelings, tell ourselves these feelings will not benefit our enlightenment, and then let them pass on. If we just allow ourselves to be angry or depressed, then we're going to stay that way. But if we ask ourselves when those emotions arise "Why am I getting angry? Why am I depressed? " then we have a better chance of overcoming those emotions and getting to the root cause of our suffering.

I have so much pain and stress from all the relationships I've been in. I feel like being in a relationship or loving someone always end up giving me such agony. From what I've studied, love isn't spoken much in Buddhism. Are we better off being alone so that we won't be vulnerable enough for others to hurt us? Where does Buddhism stand when it comes to love and relationship?

Buddhism is all about love and compassion, the two words are sometimes used interchangeably, but Buddhism definitely emphasizes love, because we can't win with violence and anger, only with love and kindness.

We don't have to be alone. The Buddha said that we didn't have to renounce the world, our family, or friends to be on the path to enlightenment, that's why he shared his teachings with everyone because everyone has the possibility to attain enlightenment, whether layperson or monastic.

The reason people hurt us, cause us suffering, pain, agony, etc., is because we let them. In Buddhism there's no blame, we don't blame others – we're the only person to blame for our suffering. Why? Because we allowed that person to hurt us. Just because they broke up with us or hurt our feelings, they didn't do anything wrong. What was wrong is we allowed ourselves to attach to them and let our ego depend on them, so if something went wrong or ended, we're the one to suffer.

Attachment is one of the main causes of suffering. We attach to people, our cars, houses, electronics, etc. We're saddened when they leave or break because we think we *need* them. We don't need anything. All we need is ourselves. Only we can make us happy. This isn't easy. Getting over attachment is extremely difficult because we're curious, social animals, and we're always going to want the newest gadgets, a big group of friends, people to want/love us, a nice car and house, etc. So the best thing to do is try to lessen the *need* for things and people. If we think we just *have* to have a Starbucks every day, try cutting down a day every week. Or if we go grocery shopping and have to have the best stuff and only buy brand products, try not to (because sometimes they're (off-brand) even better!), And eventually we can work with the notion of not having to *have* someone in our life. Because once we stop feeling sad and stop suffering because one of our favorite things broke, our car broke down, a friend moved away, or someone broke up with us – when these things don't cause us to suffer too much, we'll be a much happier person.

It's extremely important that we remember everything is impermanent. Everything will age, wither away, break and end. Everyone will grow old, get sick and die. So even if we found our "soul mate," got married and spent the rest of our lives together, we're still going to suffer. Because we're still going to age, get sick and die. If our partner dies first, that's suffering for us. If we die first, that's suffering for them. There's no exit. But routinely meditating on impermanence will greatly help us. Everything will eventually die. Even tall, strong buildings will eventually collapse. Even rocks will eventually wither away from water and air. Nothing will last, so when we finally truly realize that, after every breakup, heartache, or death, it'll be easier for us to be mindful of the impermanence of those things and know that they were bound to end eventually.

How do Buddhists deal with depression? Has the Buddha ever talked about overcoming feelings of sadness and despair?

Feelings are something we create, so naturally it's something we can destroy. Obviously, it's easier said than done, but we can overcome these feelings through meditation and contemplation. What's making us sad? Why are we in despair? We should keep asking ourselves, "Why, why, why?" for every answer that comes up until we get to the core of it; the truth. Sometimes it's the dumbest or most mundane things that cause us sadness. Maybe our friend never texted or called us back; this makes us feel lonely and sad. But why? Why do we feel we're so important that a simple thing causes us to suffer? Ego. Our ego is big enough to fill a football field, and so we let that much space of our egotistical selves control our feelings.

When we get to the core, to the truth, we'll laugh because we'll see that there is really no reason to be sad at all. As Buddhists, we understand that everything is impermanent, nothing lasts forever, including our feelings, so why should we hold on and cling to them? It only causes us to suffer, and we become depressed and unhappy. Life is precious and joyful. With a clear and peaceful mind, we can be happy regardless of what our external circumstances may be. Practice daily meditation.

As I continue to read more into Buddhism my life has been opening up in every way but in some ways/departments confusing. Compassion has been

very difficult lately. My ex-girlfriend wants to be my "friend." In the past she wasn't a good "friend," therefore, I wish to keep my distance from her. Then past couple of nights I've been exposed to some friends who have been acting very "not" so lady like. I'm turned off and find it difficult to be around any of it. How should I handle this?

The obvious answer is as obvious as the problem. If someone is chasing us, what do we do? We run! As we grow older, become wiser, and more experienced, a lot of changes will occur in our life. The most absolute are the coming and going of friends. Our friends in high school probably won't be our friends in college. Our friends in college probably won't be our friends at our job. Our friends at our job probably won't be our friends socially (outside of work and school). And our social friends probably won't be our friends for the rest of our life.

The point is, we know what's causing us to suffer, and so we know what "fixes" that problem. Running! In a less dramatic way, we leave their presence and any other toxic people. One of the eight sufferings[22] is being with those we dislike. So the answer is obvious: don't be with them! Sometimes we have to unfriend people when we

---

[22] Suffering of birth, old age, sickness, death, separating from loved ones, associating with those we dislike, unfulfilled wishes and desires, and flourishing of the five aggregates.

take the Buddhist precepts (if we vow to stop drinking/taking intoxicants), because, for many people, the basis of their friendships is drinking and partying! It's hard and sometimes sad, but we have to put in the will, effort, determination, and devotion to awakening our mind, and that means abandoning things and people that are distracting and unnecessary.

On the other hand, dealing with difficult people can be a tough challenge to practice our compassion and loving-kindness. Sometimes our job is a daily challenge to our practice. Sometimes we win, sometimes we fail. But at least, when we fail, we know we failed and we can better ourselves next time. And eventually, we'll have more wins than fails, and the toughest and most difficult of people will cross our way, and we'll be able to see and feel their pain and want nothing more than to show them love.

If I am Buddhist, and I meditate, and I do everything why do I still fail to reach complete happiness?

Reach. This verb is sometimes used a lot when reading Buddhist topics. To the ordinary person, a verb is an action word; walk, run, jump, etc. But in Buddhism, it's not an "action" word. It's not something you reach out for, look for, or is a destination. So. Happiness isn't something we can reach. It's not a destination on a map or a lost treasure.

To the modern world, happiness is getting the new iPhone, buying a new car or house, being asked out on a date, or finding that lost shoe. This is temporary happiness; they're impermanent. They'll eventually break, get lost and fade away, and then we'll be sad. So then where's the happiness?

Happiness, true happiness, is coming to the realization that everything is impermanent. Happiness is accepting things as they were, are and will become. It's about finding happiness and contentment in hard times. Why aren't we happy? Because we don't have all the pretty things rich people do? Do we not have a roof over our head, food to eat, a computer or cell phone, and Internet access? Do we not have family and friends that love us and care about us? What's there not to be happy about?

Have we forgotten about the poor, starving and dying children around the world? What about those whose families and friends died during the devastating hurricanes and earthquakes everywhere? We should be grateful and happy with what we have and then try to help others find their happiness.

Happiness isn't a destination. It isn't about having a boyfriend or girlfriend, or not having a large circle of friends, or not enough money. Happiness is being okay with our circumstances and situations. Meditation helps. But we have to be meditating on the right thing. Meditating on impermanence and compassion is going to help us find true happiness with all things and situations.

I feel a little hurt about someone who I ended up caring for. We were dating for only 6 months but unfortunately false information was given to her about me, and now she wants nothing to do with me. I have tried reaching out via text trying to get to the bottom of it and apologizing for all whatever it is I did because I'm clueless. I really did care about her, and she completely cut me off. I feel bad about it and been really just trying to meditate and calm my mind about it.

Be courageous. Sometimes situations or issues get worse the more we try to take control over them. The best thing to do is do nothing. It is true we might not have done anything wrong, and whether this information is true or false is no different to the "victim." The only thing they will see is us denying the truth, regardless of who is right or wrong.

81

A Buddhist person doesn't waste time or energy trying to clear their name of any false accusations. Because a Buddhist person is the only person that knows themselves more than anyone else, so whether we did something or not, the truth will always be with us. If this person knew us, really knew us, and if we've been practicing the Buddhist path, following an ethical lifestyle, practicing and sharing loving-kindness and compassion, then this truth will always shine through any falsehood that might be used against us.

If a person has any doubts whatsoever about our loyalty, no matter how little or dumb, any information "confirming" that doubt will automatically turn into a major ordeal. So it's up to us to live a life that portrays to people that we are not a person of dishonesty, disloyalty, or any bad habits, so if something negative or untrue was told about us, no one would believe it.

Do nothing. Show people that we know the truth. The more we go after it, the more people are going to assume we're trying to cover our tracks and cover up the "truth." Courage and self-confidence will get us through it. Meditate on it and practice it, and people will see that beauty and light.

How do I develop true happiness?

It is everyone's life mission to be happy. Every sentient being wants happiness and a good life. And so it is also our life's mission to develop that happiness, for and from ourselves, from within. It is unfortunate that we live in a world where society has brainwashed us that new, pretty, fancy things will bring us happiness. That our life would be incomplete without the latest trending gadgets, cars, clothes, and even foods. We spend hundreds and thousands of dollars to be part of the status-quo, to fit in, and make sure we're on the same trending page as the rest of the world.

Are we happy with all that? Yes, for a hot minute. Only until the next latest gadget is released, next year's model car is for sale, and the new season clothing line has come and gone before we've even realized it exists. We have this completely false assumption that these "things" bring us real happiness, that they have this magical way of taking all our dissatisfactions of the world away, because they don't.

Real happiness is when we realize these nice things are impermanent, and the happiness they bring is also impermanent. New technology is constantly changing and developing; it can't even catch up to itself. With a blink of an eye the new iPhone is released, the next thing we know, the iPhone is going to be a tiny chip we have to embed in our heads!

83

Buddhism is not a fixing path; it's a healing path. If we come into Buddhism assuming it's going to magically fix all our life problems, then we are the problem in our life. Buddhism gives us the guidelines and instructions to understanding life and our minds, and to use those instructions to help us escape what we see as dissatisfying as a different view of reality. By understanding life (using the Four Noble Truths) and following the guidelines of the Eightfold Path, we start understanding our mind and the world around us and why things cause us dissatisfaction.

By understanding and learning how our dissatisfaction arises and where it comes from, we can start eradicating those causes for dissatisfaction and start living our lives happily. Happiness isn't entirely caused by eradicating the bad things, but by understanding that there are bad things and bad things can and will happen. So when they do, it is our responsibility to take that opportunity to go back to our practice and focus on the issue - What is the situation? How are we feeling? What are we feeling? Is that how we really want to feel? What can we do to change the situation/feeling in a positive way?

It's important that when anger or any other negative feeling arises, that we take a moment to breathe, concentrate on our breathing, and know that the feeling will pass. It's our job to take and make any negative situation or feeling into a positive one. We can do that by reminding ourselves of our practice, of the Dharma, or even by remembering loved ones or good memories. We can also take the time to realize just how fortunate we are to others. We might think our lives suck because we don't have or make a lot of money, don't have many friends or things just don't go our way. But there are many, many people out there with far less than we do or with nothing at all. We might not have a lot or everything we want, but we, at least, have a home, family and friends, the internet, and the ability and accessibility of learning and practicing the Dharma.

Happiness isn't out there or with things. Happiness is with ourselves and the way we look at things.

"You'll never see the beauty in a chaotic world if all you're doing is looking at the disasters instead of the sprouting flowers underneath the fallen tree." - Quang Trí.

I struggle the most with compassion, forgiveness, anger, and trust. (raised in a religious cult by military-type household nearly ended my life). Also tolerance. I know I can't go on without it but what are some other ways to cultivate a healthy mindset

***with these characteristics at the forefront? It is
extremely hard for me, and I want to be better.***

Sometimes during our practice of compassion,
forgiveness, getting over anger, etc., we think we have to
cultivate these attitudes for others, but we really need to
establish these characteristics for ourselves first.

It's important to have compassion and forgive
others, but we have to have compassion and forgive
ourselves first. How can we help others escape their
struggles and suffering if we can't do it for ourselves?
There have always been seeds of anger, hate, mistrust,
ignorance and greed that's been planted in our
consciousness, and it takes the right circumstances for
them to grow and flourish. Often it's the situations in our
own lives growing up; whether it's family issues or
personal issues.

As adults, we should have a content understanding
that "stuff happens" and if we want things to change,
then we must change them by our own efforts and
diligence. If you want good grades in school, study
harder. If you want a better job, work harder. If you want
to spiritually awaken, then you must put in the effort to
overcome your ignorance, greed and anger.

Meditate. Contemplate on the things that anger you.
Contemplate on why they anger you and why you allow
them to anger you. What good is letting someone or

something anger you? Is it helping you in your life? In others' lives? Is your anger helping you enlighten yourself?

Meditate on compassion, love and forgiveness for yourself. Once you're able to emancipate yourself from your own blocking walls and help yourself, then you can start helping others. Your happiness and peace can help others, and others' happiness is your own happiness.

Tips for dealing with recurring depression and reasons to live?

Depression happens for many internal reasons; it doesn't just spontaneously happen. Depression occurs when we allow certain life situations to take over us, and then our brains start having a techno-house party and moves some chemicals around to create this imbalance that creates depression, anxiety, and other mental stuff.

There are dozens of studies out there now that show that meditation and mindfulness can really help with depression and anxiety. An important lesson to know is that we are not our thoughts. Ronald Siegel, an Assistant Professor of Psychology at Harvard Medical School, defines mindfulness as "awareness of the present experience with acceptance."

That's a pretty accurate and awesome definition, I think. But then we might say, "I'm aware, I'm present, I'm accepting," but we're really not. We're not aware, we're staring at our computer screens. We're not present; we're worrying about the future. We're not accepting, we're cussing out people or drivers on the road.

Being mindful is taking the world around us in and being aware of it, but we're not doing that. We're listening to the stories we tell ourselves about the world and how we want it to be, instead of actually paying attention to life around us.

We all take our thoughts way too seriously. We have this crazy notion that our thoughts actually mean something. We think we are our thoughts, and our thoughts are us. That's why we suffer so much and experience negative emotions – because we take our thoughts about the world more seriously than the world itself. These thoughts range from thinking someone loves/hates us, no one caring about us, to thinking you're the most attractive person on campus – none of which may or may not be true unless we're truly aware of the world around us.

Why are you depressed? Why do you want to take your life? Life is absolutely beautiful, but you have to choose to see it as it is. Our world is full of anger, greed, chaos and destruction, but it is also filled with gorgeous mountains, forests, gardens, oceans and people

– things that are only on this planet. We might not have the most fabulous life, I mean does anyone really anyway – but, at least, we are alive, are well and have the capability and choice to change our lives to make it better. "I can't" is not a valid excuse if you think you don't have the means to do something.

If you want to go to college but can't afford it, get a job and work your way to it or apply for scholarships, grants or loans. There is a means and a way for everything, it's our job to be diligent to find the way. If we give up on our first or second try, the world didn't give up on us, we gave up on us – and that's not going to make us stronger. If you want to get over depression, face your fears and your feelings, conquer them and move on.

Be mindful of your thoughts. Ask yourself, "is this real or am I just making it up?" If someone angers you, don't get angry back, instead laugh at them and remind yourself that the words they say are not who/what you are. If I called you ugly, does that actually, literally, physically make you ugly? No! So why would it matter what I said, just acknowledge it, laugh it off and move on. When we become mindful of our thoughts, we can then meditate on them to dig deeper into the real core causes of our feelings. We don't just randomly become depressed. There was something that triggered our depression that we allowed to happen inside ourselves, and now we have to find what that was and eliminate it.

How do I not let everything get to me? I have a friend who I think is no longer my friend just a fake one. I've tried making new friends, but I'm finding it really hard. Do you have any strategies on how to stay positive and not let the little things get to me?

Compassion. Compassion towards ourselves is very important. Losing friends and growing apart from friends as the years go by is natural. Every best friend I've grown up with, I am no longer in contact with. The people that knew me better than myself are no longer in my life. And that's okay. That's impermanence. It's inevitable.

When we were kids, making friends was a piece of cake. We would bond instantly because we liked the same color Crayon. As we get older, and we grow into our personalities, our likes, and dislikes, habits, biases, etc., we start getting picky of who we want to bond with and who we don't. So naturally, it's harder to make new friends.

I never really had a big group of friends, but I socialized a lot, so I knew a lot of people. I'm naturally an introvert and a hermit at heart. I prefer staying in and reading a book than going out and be surrounded by uncomfortable crowds. Making friends as adults is stressful and time-consuming because there's actually effort involved! But it's not impossible. Some of my best friends today are people I met at work and at the temple I go to, and at volunteer events.

For anything to happen in our lives, whether it's making friends, building a birdhouse, growing a garden, or cooking dinner – it takes effort and dedication. If all we do is mope around and wish we were happy when we're miserable, then we have no one to blame but ourselves! You want a better, a happier life then get up and do something about it! Life is not passive, it's active, you actually have to work for it. Life is like a plant; we have to water it, give it sun and nurture it so it can grow and flourish into the beauty that it's meant to be!

I just started studying Buddhism about a year ago. I'm a middle-aged man, and I've been through a lot this past year. My problem is letting go of my anger and resentment. It seems the more I strive to overcome it, the more powerful it becomes. How can I break this cycle and allow more peaceful energy into my life?

Our anger is like a child. The more we tell them to settle down and be quiet, the wilder and more hyped up they get. Likewise, the more we try to suppress and "control" our anger, the harder it is to actually overcome it because we end up just getting angrier because nothing is "working."

So instead of trying to go at our anger with more anger and control, we need to approach it with compassion, understanding and contemplation. It's important to sit down in meditation and meditate on self-compassion so we don't get angry at ourselves when trying to overcome anger.

When we contemplate and approach our anger, we don't try to push it out, we do the opposite. We contemplate on why we're angry and then try to eliminate the causes that create that anger so that it doesn't always return when those causes arise again. If all we're doing is trying to get rid of getting angry instead of what's getting us angry, then the anger will never really go away.

So continue meditating. Look past the superficial reasons of why we're angry. Dig deeper and deeper until you can find the core reason and causes that create the anger in the first place. Then work on those causes, either by eliminating them or working with them so that they don't always have to cause anger.

I know that in Buddhism, parents are to be highly respected because they are our first Dharma teachers in this current life. However, that doesn't seem to be the case for some of us. What if my parents have been teaching and forcing me to practice Adharma instead? What if there are many of traumas my parents have caused me? Say, teaching & forcing me to lie, to hate & be violent, they literally spat on my face, they beat me every day and once I was forced to get out of the house naked, etc.

When we practice Buddhism, we practice everything with compassion. That is how we show people the correct way – by example, not by force. It is true that some parents are not fit to be parents at all, that they should have never had children in the first place. However, deep down inside they still have to love their children. Otherwise, they could have easily aborted or given the child up for adoption or simply just left somewhere.

As children there is not much we can do to abstain from the things our parents force us to do, it seems like we would always be on the losing side. As we get older and become adults, we have the power, attitude and patience to help teach our parents.

Since most parents as we've become adults are probably set in their ways, views, opinions, discrimination, biases, etc., it would seem nearly impossible to "change" their mind. But we don't want to change their mind. Instead, we need to show and teach them right view and right understanding. Even though they might have caused us great suffering as children, we need to do the exact opposite for them. Show them compassion and love, help them with chores and bills, show them that their attempt at cruelty and suffering has failed and that you have forgiven them. They need to help themselves, *for* themselves.

One of my favorite Buddhist stories is of Maudgalyayana and his mother. When Maudgalyayana attained enlightenment, he saw his mother in hell as a hungry ghost because she was cruel and slandered monks, giving them dog meat as alms. Maudgalyayana was deeply saddened and tried to go to her and offer her food, but for every bite she tried to consume, it would go up in flames, not allowing her to eat.

Maudgalyayana asked the Buddha what he could do to save his mother. The Buddha advised that his mother had to change by her own will, but that he should pray for her. So Maudgalyayana and 99 other monks prayed for her for 100 days. Hearing her son's prayers, the mother felt her son's deep compassion and love, so she repented and vowed to become a better person. She got out of hell and was reborn in a heavenly realm.

So like the story of Maudgalyayana and his mother, we must equally do the same for our parents. Praying for them and showing them great compassion. Through our own efforts and intentions, we can help our parents see the right view and right understanding.

I've recently been extremely interested in the teachings of Buddha. I've been doing research on such things, and I don't know what the first step should be. But I have so much pain and suffering in my heart and mind, and I just want to live happily. I've been teaching myself to meditate but would really like some help because my mind always wanders.

A lot of people, and I mean *a lot* of people, misunderstand what Buddhism really is. Externally, it looks like the perfect "peace-centered" religion with all the people being "Buddhists" looking and seeming like they're on cloud nine and happy as can be. Oh, the ignorance.

Buddhism is not a happy pill. No religion is a happy pill. The only way we can get happy pills is with a prescription! Every religion (for the most part) preaches love and peace, if we dig past all the bias and politics, it's been feeding society over hundreds of years. Every religion has their own form of liberation and the means of attaining it. Most religions are about devotion and worship to a god or deity, and that is supposed to give you faith and happiness.

In Buddhism, it's the complete opposite. Buddhism is non-faith-based. Meaning your faith or worship in Buddha is not going to get you any closer to liberation than your faith or worship in God. Buddhism is a mind-centered, self-help religion. So the only faith and worship we need is in ourselves. We can pray to God for a better life with less suffering all we want, but we have to go out there and do it ourselves if we want a better life!

Buddhism is like a toolbox, and our lives are like a house we want to build. Buddhism provides all the tools we need to hammer in nails, measure wood for cutting and paint to finish the house. When we're done building, we no longer need the tools, so we either put them away or give them to someone else who needs them. Likewise, Buddhism provides us with the tools, the teachings, to help us build our lives to a better, more "finished" outcome; enlightenment.

When we've attained enlightenment, or near it, we then use the tools/teachings to help others attain enlightenment as well. Buddhism has many tools (schools/traditions of Buddhism) for us to pick and choose from depending on what we want and how we want to use it.

Regardless, we must always start with the basics. And meditation is not about clearing our mind, otherwise the more you try to force the thoughts from coming, the more they'll fight back. Instead, we meditate to observe and become aware of our thoughts while not entertaining or feeding the thoughts. Eventually, the thoughts will lessen.

Part IV

Meditation and Mindfulness

How Can I Keep Concentration During Meditation?

Meditation and concentration are emphasized in almost every Buddhist introductory book, as well as in many sutras. For good reason, too. Concentration leads to wisdom, and that wisdom can lead us to Nirvana. Unless we're a monk or a nun, we probably don't have several hours a day to meditate and develop that much-needed concentration. Regardless, meditation should be a daily routine, even if it's just for 10-15 minutes. Scientifically,[23] meditation can help us release stress, anxiety, depression and anger, but it can also help us cultivate our loving-kindness, compassion, equanimity, and of course, concentration.

Besides meditating for the benefits above, Buddhists

---

[23] "Meditation: A simple, fast way to reduce stress." Mayo Clinic. http://www.mayoclinic.org.

practice meditation to contemplate on sutras, topics, mantras, or to simply look deeply within themselves to discover their Buddha Nature[24]. With strong dedication and practice, we will be able to transcend to higher levels of consciousness and climb to higher stages of meditation[25]. Our goal in meditation is to reach a level of deep concentration, Samadhi. Samadhi is one-pointed concentration. This means concentrating on one object for the whole duration of our meditation with minimal to no distractions. We can concentrate on our breath, an image, a statue, a candle flame, or a mantra. The point is not to let anything else distract us from that one object. Once Samadhi is perfected, we can reach Samatha; the quiet, calmness, and tranquility of our mind.

There are many different ways to concentrate. The best and easiest way is to concentrate on our breath. Anapanasati,[26] mindfulness of breathing, is the practice

---

[24] Buddha Nature is a central feature of Mahayana Buddhism. It refers to the notion that all sentient beings possess the potential to become Buddhas. Also referred to as *Tathāgatagarbha* and *Buddha-dhātu*.

[25] The Nine Levels of Meditation, or Nine Stages of Training the Mind, are the stages of consciousness, which equate to the nine qualities of concentrated attention.

[26] A meditation exercise to feel the sensations in the body caused by the movement of the breath and to be mindful of it.

of observing our breath as it goes in and out. Or by counting our breaths, whichever works best. Here's one exercise:

Sit down in a quiet place and take a couple of minutes to settle the breath. Then, feel your breath going in and out of the tip of the nose. Feel the air move against the inside of the nose, feel it go "in" and "out" and say it in your mind; "in" and "out" as you feel it against your nose. Do this 3-5 times. Then feel the air go "in" and "out" at the back of your mouth at the entrance of the throat. Feel the air move "in" and "out," feel its warmth or coldness, concentrate on that area and feel the air. Do this for another 3-5 times.

Next, move on to the throat/neck. Feel the air go "in" and "out" of the throat. Feel it move up and down. Feel its warmth or its coldness. Concentrate on that area and feel it going "in" and "out." Do this 3-5 times. Next, feel the "in" and "out" breath go into the lungs. Feel the lungs expand with air and feel it contract. Feel the air go "in" and "out." Do this 3-5 times.

Then, breathe "in" and "out" for the whole body. Feel your entire body being absorbed by the air you're breathing. Next, move backwards from your lungs, your throat/neck, back of your mouth, to your nose – again 3-5 times each. And then repeat.

This is a great way to focus on concentration. By concentrating on one thing at a time, but having multiple "one things" to concentrate on, it helps not to bore us as quickly versus just concentrating on the breath the whole time. If we repeat the exercise 3-5 times (depending on how slow or fast we breathe), that's our 10-minute daily meditation right there!

How do I become mindful?

Mindfulness is a pretty important routine. When we're mindful of our thoughts, speech, and actions, we can do great things or stop bad things from happening. The practice of mindfulness is to simply acknowledge the things we're doing; walking, eating, driving, doing dishes, putting the laundry away, showering, etc. Mindfulness is also very important during meditation. Without mindfulness during meditation, our whole session will be filled with distracting and entertaining thoughts.

It's understandable that it's extremely difficult to be mindful of *everything* we do in our daily, busy, hectic lives. The trick is to be at least aware of mindfulness. We probably won't be noting every little thing we do like lifting, pushing, writing, pouring coffee, drinking, talking, sighing, opening/closing doors, or even breathing! We'd have to be extremely skilled to be able to be mindful and note of every movement, action, thought, and breath all day, every day. It's almost impossible. However, what we *can* do is, at least, be mindful of the basics; walking, drinking, eating, moving, and when we can, breathing. We'll get plenty of distractions throughout the day, but whenever we can remind ourselves to be mindful. Eventually with practice, we'll be able to be more mindful of more things and less effort.

When we meditate, it's important to note any thoughts that arise. When a thought arises, simply note it as "thinking, thinking" and it'll go away on its own. If an emotion arises, try to categorize the emotion and note it, whether it's anger, jealousy, sadness, or whatever other emotion. Even when the body starts getting discomforted or sore, note "discomfort, discomfort." Even these discomforting feelings, like the feeling of your leg or foot falling asleep, will go away. In the meantime, be mindful of your breath by noting the "in and out" of the breath, by counting the breath as "1, 1. 2, 2. 3, 3…," or by the rise and fall of the abdomen. Thoughts will arise, but when they do, quickly note them, and they will go away. With practice, fewer and fewer thoughts will arise until none arise at all.

I'm a little lazy with my meditation practice. I have a strong desire to want to practice, but sometimes I just get tired and bored.

Meditation laziness is not that uncommon for people who don't have a strong, disciplined practice. We can have all the motivation in the world to want to meditate, but unless we have a strong, disciplined practice, we'll always suffer from meditation laziness.

Meditation laziness happens because our concentration is weak. Meditation is all about our concentration and the amount of energy and focus we put into our concentration. If we can concentrate correctly, it will take little effort to concentrate, but for beginners or weak-disciplined practitioners, finding and holding onto that concentration can seem impossible.

It's true, meditation can sometimes become boring if we're not using the right technique. There are a plethora of techniques, exercises, and practices to do for meditation, so we just have to find the one that works for us and master it. The most common technique, especially in Buddhist practice, is Anapanasati (mindful breathing). Whether we are noting our in and out breaths or counting our breaths, the practice of mindful breathing is an important one. Because breathing is something we just automatically do, we never notice or realize when we are breathing heavy, breathing shallowly, breathing long or short breaths, so when we sit and meditate on our breath, we are able to understand our breathing and become aware of it.

Meditation is also about awareness. Our concentration feeds our awareness, and our awareness feeds our concentration. When we sit to meditate, we can move our focus from our breath to the sounds we hear. Not only the sounds of our body, but also the sounds of our environment; the clock ticking, birds chirping, cars moving, people walking, dogs barking, thunder roaring, or rain dropping. Every time we hear a sound, be aware of it and note the sound. Don't go after the sound and wonder where it's coming from, who or what it is, simply acknowledge the sound and go back to sitting there being aware of any other sounds we hear.

Another thing we can do is contemplation. Once a certain degree of concentration has been reached in our meditation practice, we should then start contemplation. Contemplation can be about anything whether suffering, the four noble truths, loving-kindness, compassion, bodhicitta, death—anything. Contemplation leads to further understanding, wisdom, and insight into whatever we're contemplating on. Mantra chanting is another form we can try. Chanting out loud helps us keep our concentration on our own voice, so wandering thoughts and distractions are less likely to happen, but still can. Mantra chanting can be of anything – an actual Buddhist

mantra like the six-syllable mantra,[27] the Medicine
Buddha mantra[28], Sakyamuni Buddha mantra,[29] or
simply "OM." Or you can simply make anything up or
use a random word like "car," "dog" or literally anything
else. The point isn't about what you're saying, but that
your focus and concentration stays one-pointed with what
you're saying.

How do I keep away from unwanted sensual thoughts? Whenever I try to meditate such thoughts, disturb me.

Practice, practice, practice! Keeping unwanted
thoughts away isn't easy, and it takes time to even notice
them and to get the number of thoughts to decrease. It's
important to be mindful of when these thoughts arise, so
when they do, we simply acknowledge the thought and
simply move on without engaging with it. What keeps
meditation full of distractions is the engagements we

---

[27] The Compassion Mantra is also known as the six-syllable
mantra of Avalokitesvara. It is "Om Mani Padme Hum."

[28] The short version of the Medicine Buddha mantra is "*Oṃ
bhaiṣajye bhaiṣajye bhaiṣajya-samudgate svāhā.*"

[29] "Namo Sakyamuni Buddha"

have with our thoughts. We might not realize it at first, but even when we're trying to concentrate on something like our breath or a mantra, a thought always seems to arise, and we'll almost always engage with it.

So, when concentrating on the breath and a thought arises, we need to try as quickly as possible to be mindful that the thought has risen and take ourselves back to our breath. It will take time, but eventually we'll get to a point where we'll be able to catch the rising thoughts as soon as they arise, and then the thoughts will lessen, then maybe we'll get one or two thoughts, and finally a calm mind. Again, this will take much practice, but with daily meditation, it's very possible and doable.

I've been a Buddhist for almost a year now, but I have a problem with cursing. I meditate on it all the time and try my hardest not to, but I slip up when I'm around other people. Any suggestions?

I'm sure a lot of people can relate that when in certain situations say horrible things that we would never say around our mother, but it happens. But, because we know we're going to slip up, and we know in what situations cause us to slip, this gives us an opportunity to be able to stop it before it happens.

Mindfulness is key here. This is where we can fully practice, watch our practice, correct it and perfect it. It's not easy. It'll take practice. But whenever we're in a situation where we feel like we're about to curse, remind ourselves to stop, think, breathe and let it go before the words ever utter our lips.

When we're able to stop ourselves from cursing, ask, "What is cursing accomplishing? Will it get me to my destination any quicker? Will it make the person dumber? Will it make me feel any better?" The answer is always going to be no! Calling someone stupid doesn't make them stupid. They're only stupid if they accept they're stupid. Who are we to call them stupid? If someone called us fat and ugly does that make us fat and ugly? No. What authority, power, or influence does that person have to call us anything and make us believe it? Depression, anxiety, fear, sadness, etc. is usually no one's fault but our own. If something bad or sad happens, the only way it'll affect us negatively is if we allow it to.

Like anything else we want to do and learn, it takes time and patience. Just because we want to stop cursing doesn't mean we can just automatically turn that switch off. It takes time, practice, compassion and loving-kindness to cut through the "reason" we curse in the first place. Eventually, it'll get down to a minimum before it stops completely.

Just remember always to breathe and stay mindful. Everything starts as a thought, so before that thought becomes words or actions, make sure it's a good, virtuous thought.

Do you have to be a Buddhist to practice meditation? My sister says so, and she says that if I do, I'm not staying true to my religion and such. Also, can you be Buddhist and Christian?

What is meditation? It's simply a practice of concentration and focusing our mind on one thing. So if we think about it, a lot of what we do on a daily basis is meditation! Driving, taking a shower, getting ready, working, etc., everything we do that has one objective can be considered meditation. Prayer is also a form of meditation! A lot of Christians meditate on prayer because it's calming, relaxing, and eases their mind.

So no, we don't have to be Buddhist to meditate. General meditation has nothing to do with Buddhism. On the other hand, practicing Buddhism – not being Buddhist, but just practicing the teachings of compassion, loving-kindness, appreciative joy, and equanimity will make us a better person and a better practitioner of our own religion.

109

So go ahead and practice meditation all you want! With practice, we will discover that it will bring us closer to ourselves and to God.

I am doing meditation for quite some time now. Every day I meditate for 10-15mins. But still I have not felt any progress or the inner peace and tranquil that comes from meditation. On the contrary, I feel more lonely and have become disinterested in all the social and worldly activities. I like now to spend time in meditation and reading scriptures or books by great masters. Please, could you explain how to progress in meditation?

We're not going to gain anything from meditation. But we will lose the things that make us want to meditate (depression, anger, hatred, ignorance, etc.). From meditation, we develop concentration, wisdom, compassion, and learn to center ourselves so we can ultimately free ourselves completely from the worldly poisons of ignorance, anger and greed.

Don't meditate thinking we're going to be peaceful and blissful only during meditation, then having to go back to the "real world" that's full of suffering. Meditation's ultimate goal is to allow us to be at peace and bliss in the real world of suffering. It is only then that we can be at a heightened level of peace during meditation. From then we work on an even higher level of concentration to develop the wisdom to free ourselves from Samsara.

We will need to meditate for a little longer than 10-15 minutes. Especially if we've been at it for some time. 10-15 minutes is good for beginning meditators for the first 1-6 months, but as we develop our meditation, our time needs to increase. Add an extra five minutes to our usual time, and then add five-minute increments as we feel comfortable.

The *Nine Levels of Meditation* is an excellent guide to help us progress in meditation. Though it might take a whole lifetime or many lifetimes to achieve a greater level, it is still a guide worth referring to.

Meditate with the intention of gaining nothing, but developing our compassion, acceptance, generosity, and concentration. This is what will create our peace and bliss, and make both our life and meditation sessions peaceful and happy.

Lately, I've been feeling really chaotic, and it's messed up my grades. I've tried yoga and meditation, but as soon as I go into study, I feel like my head is full and can't be emptied, despite what I

did before. I'm also afraid that I won't succeed, so I don't feel like trying. In terms of emptying myself of all these feelings and being more concentrated, what should I do?

Continue meditating. Yoga only tames the body, but meditation tames the mind (though I'm sure many will argue that yoga also tames the mind, whatever works for you). Meditation, or any activity to clear our mind, is not a one-time, miracle pill; you have to take several doses before it has any real effect on you. With meditation, it takes endless practice and a lifetime to be able to sit with a clear mind and have the hours go by as if they were only seconds.

Giving up on studying is not going to make you study or bring up your grades. If you want good grades, then you have to work hard to get them. If you want an "empty" mind, then you have to work hard to achieve it. Nothing happens for you because you simply "want" it. We're not gods; we can't just snap our fingers and have things magically happen.

You must meditate with diligence, effort, and a strong will to achieve a peaceful, clear mind. 5-10 minutes a day is not going to cut it. It takes 15 minutes just to get into a mindset that is only slightly wavy with thoughts. If you're only beginning meditation, you can start with 10-15 minutes for a couple of weeks or months, but then you should start increasing your time with 3-5 minute increments.

Just keep meditating. Concentrate on something that makes you happy or smile. When you study, concentrate on why you're studying; to get good grades, graduate with a high GPA, get a great job and live a life with little worries.

What's the best way to meditate on my breath?

Meditation is an essential part of Buddhist practice. Breathing is an essential part of meditation practice (and obviously to stay alive!). There are myriad of techniques of concentrating during meditation, but the most common and traditional is concentrating on our breath.

Our breath is the most powerful tool to concentrate on and keep our focus. Other techniques are focusing on an image, statue, a sound, or visualization, but these methods can easily make us lose our concentration once a distracting thought or incident arises. The easiest breathing method is counting our breath; count 1 for every inhale-exhale and continue counting until we reach 10, then start over. If we become distracted or lose count, begin again from 1.

As we progress with this method, we can increase the increments from 10 to 20 and so forth, until we reach a stage where we can easily reach 100 or 1000 without any distractions. Don't just count our breath, feel the air go in and out of the nose, feel our abdomen and chest rise and fall – because if we're just boringly counting, we will be distracted by thoughts and lose our concentration.

To help us get ready for our breath counting exercise, we can first begin to "relax our breath." If we have a clock, or, at least, a sound of a ticking clock in the background (I'm sure there's an app for that), this will help us with this exercise.

To begin: make sure we're in a relaxed and comfortable position. Meditation doesn't require any specific method of seating or position, just be comfortable to avoid too much movement. With the sound of the clock, we're going to take quick, short breaths – inhale for 1 second, exhale for 1 second, doing one each for every second. Let's do this for about 1 minute.

Next, inhale and exhale for 2 seconds each. Again, do this for about 1 minute. Finally, inhale and exhale for 3 seconds each for about 1 minute. After this exercise, our breath should be relaxed, light and semi-short. This is where and how our breathing should be for meditation. From there we can begin our breath counting exercise; focusing on the air that's going in and out of our nose, and the rising and falling of our abdomen and chest.

If distractions do arise, our counting will most likely get lost, and we will have to start over. This is not a bad thing because we want to know that we've become distracted. Often times many thoughts and scenarios will pop in our head, and we don't notice for several seconds or minutes, and our meditation has been wasted. But when we are counting, and we get distracted and lose count, then we will immediately know and remind ourselves to go back to our breath and counting. Eventually, our mind will begin to retain itself to lessen distracting and unwanted thoughts, and we will begin having a clear mind and blissful meditations.

I have been working on my meditation, but I want to take it further. What advice do you have for meditating with a mala? And what are some chants I can do?

The only use for a mala is to keep count, whether it's your breath or mantras. You can do any chants or mantras. You can even make one up if you want.

Mantras/chants during meditation serve one of two (or even both) purposes: 1) To help you keep your focus and concentration on what you're chanting. The stronger your focus is on the chant, the less likely you'll have distracting thoughts. 2) To help you contemplate on the purpose behind the chant. Most mantras/chants are invocations or praises to Buddhas or Bodhisattvas, so there's not much to contemplate there. But others have a deeper meaning like *Om Mani Padme Hum*, which, though short and "simple," is quite profound and deep.

There are hundreds of different mantras or chants you can do. You just have to find one that you feel a connection to. Or you can stay simple and chant the three universal sounds "Om Ah Hum."

Advancing in meditation is different for different people. It depends on what you're wanting to accomplish. Are you trying to enter a state of peace? Are you trying to prolong your meditation into 1, 2, 3 or 4-hour sessions? Are you meditating to obtain insight into the true nature of reality? What are you trying to do? You can't do it all at once, so you need to make a decision on how you're trying to advance.

Whatever path you choose to go, there are some prerequisites you will need to master first. 1) Mastering your breath. Can you count to 100 without any distraction or losing count? 2) Mastering your posture. Can you meditate for the duration of your session without having to readjust your back/posture? 3) Mastering your peace. Can you meditate for the duration of your session without any or too many thoughts/distractions? 4) Mastering your time. Can you meditate for 1 hour, 2 hours?

Until your answer is yes to all those
questions, "advance" meditation cannot be achieved.
However, during your practice of mastering all those
prerequisites, you can practice contemplation (insight
meditation) on certain "enlightening" topics in Buddhism
like the twelve links of dependent origination and
the four noble truths. Once everything is mastered, then
you can begin meditating on emptiness if you want to
achieve enlightenment, or meditate on nothing if you
want bliss.

***I wouldn't really consider myself a Buddhist since I
just started practicing it four weeks ago. But ever
since I've been reading more about the subject,
plus reading your blog every day has made me
think that this will be the way for me to achieve
peace in my soul. But since I have a bad temper,
people tend to cross the line a lot and make me not
have inner peace anymore. My question to you is
how can you maintain to have that inner peace in
you?***

Practice and meditation. By no means am I all
peaceful and blissful inside. 50% of the time I have crazy
road rage and wish I had super powers to blast everyone
on the road. Obviously, that's not very Buddhist, *BUT*

there's a very important practice when it comes to overcoming anger – mindfulness.

With mindfulness, or at least by practicing mindfulness, we can take each thought, speech and action step-by-step and watch them. By keeping aware of what we're thinking, saying and doing, we can quickly notice any positive or negative feelings or emotions about to arise and stop the negative ones before they turn into harmful words or actions.

There are a lot of instances where we go in knowing that it will cause us some sort of frustration or agitation, whether it's work, driving, or whatever. For these situations, we can "prepare" ourselves for whatever negative thoughts might arise. By knowing that these thoughts are a possibility, we can continually remind ourselves to think positively and not to allow the negativity of the situation to bother us.

Because I hate driving and people driving, I have to listen to something pleasant. If it's not good music, then I'll look something up on YouTube – usually a sutra or mantra – and listen to that. As I listen to it, it keeps my mind off the surrounding negativity that may or may not be there. So instead of getting angry at whatever situation it is – stop, take a few deep breaths, and chant something or make something up.

If it's people that are angering you, then instead of getting angry back, act back with compassion and understanding. We are all human, each and every one of us has love, anger, confusion, sadness, jealousy, greed, etc. in us – none of us are special no matter who we are. We all have bad days and good days. We cry, we bleed, we age, get sick, and we all die. We are all the same; we are all family. So why are you getting angry at family?

Think and act with compassion, not aggression. Meditate on compassion. Practice the loving-kindness meditation: meditate and wish your family happiness, freedom from suffering and their liberation. Then do the same with your friends, and then your co-workers, your acquaintances, strangers, your "enemies," and finally for all sentient beings.

I still have a few years of school and studying left to do, and I'm really attracted to the Buddhist ideology and way of life. But, I feel like it's very hard to act all calm around aggressive, negative and frustrated teenagers. My first reaction right now if someone were to say a mean and unnecessary comment or threaten to beat me up would be to do the exact same thing. But, I'm guessing that isn't very Buddhist. What should I do? Just meditate and not do anything about it?

If you did something about it, then you'll wish you didn't. But if you didn't do anything about it, you'll wish you did, so it almost seems like a lose-lose situation. No matter where you read about it, almost all Buddhist texts/teachers will say to react to everything with compassion.

Especially for teenagers and young adults, because I'm sure a majority of people who aren't in the real working adulthood world, are still going through their idiot phase, and in this idiot phase, stupid decisions are made. Unfortunately for the Western world (or anywhere, really), we are taught by example by our society, a society that is full of discrimination, violence, aggression, ignorance, greed, jealousy, fame, etc. So we live our lives based on these characteristics because that's what we know/act/treat others.

To counter the negativity, we need to fight with positivity. Instead of lashing out and fighting back and showing these people that you're just like them, you draw back and think/act with compassion – showing them that your methods of dealing are better than theirs. Western society sees compassion as a sign of weakness, but in reality, the bravest thing you can do is to show people that the best way to win a fight is with compassion and love.

Every war our Earth has ever had was because of greed, anger and discrimination. If the war-starters reacted with compassion and understanding instead, Earth would be a Utopia. We need to reorganize our society from violence, ignorance and hate, to a society of love, compassion and understanding.

The best thing you can do is to remind yourself that whenever you feel like you're about to fight back, whether with words or actions, that no good is going to come out of it. The anger and violence will still be there, and you will still have no peace of mind. What good will come out of fighting? Meditate. Lots of it. Learn a chant or mantra to recite in your head whenever difficult situations arise. Breathe deeply and bring your mind back to your breath whenever you're in those situations. Walk away and breathe mindfully.

I've just started exploring Buddhism, and I've already started to notice the changing in my thinking. However I'm having a hard time meditating, any tips?

You could be meditating for a year, and it would still be difficult. Reading a few books, watching a dozen videos or lectures on YouTube, and assuming we know how to do something, doesn't make us an expert at it.

Meditation is literally a lifetime's worth of practice. I've been meditating since 2002, and my meditation is still nowhere near perfect. But it is, however, better than when I started! Practice makes perfect, and that's all you really can do. Meditate more frequently, longer and harder – eventually, you'll be able to turn the thousands of thoughts rushing through your mind into 999 thoughts, then 998 thoughts, and so on.

One of the best and easiest practices is meditating on our breath. This is something you can do for a year or the rest of your life, but it is the most common and traditional technique for meditation.

To meditate on our breath, you simply count each in-and-out breath as 1, then count 2 for the next in-and-out breath, and so on until you reach 10, then start over. If for any reason you get distracted or lose count, you must go back and start again from 1. If you hear any distractions like a car alarm, phone ringing, etc., simply acknowledge what it is and continue with your counting. You're simply just letting your distracting thoughts know that "yes, I know you're there, I heard you, now go away," and continue counting.

After a few months, or even up to a year, of this practice, you can increase the number you're counting to. So increase the count from 10 to 15 or 20. After some time with practicing with the new number, increase the number again.

Eventually, hopefully, by keeping your focus and concentration only on your breath, and only acknowledging your thoughts and not engaging with them, your mind will wander less and less, and so should the distracting thoughts.

My book, *Making Friends With Our Mind: A Basic Guide to Buddhist Meditation*, I think, is a great introduction to some of the practices and techniques of Buddhist meditation. It'll also discuss contemplation and different levels of meditation.

I've been reading "Zen Mind, Beginners Mind" and it states that the "Full Lotus" meditation stance is key, I personally cannot get into that position (yet), so if I practice while in "Half Lotus" will I still reach the correct state of mind?

Zen Mind, Beginners Mind is one of my favorite books. Though, despite the title, it is not a very "beginners" book. Anyway. In Zen specifically, it is a very important position. It is *the* position and a necessary one. Zen is a very process-oriented, structured and disciplined practice, so the practices and rituals you do in Zen usually always has to be by the book.

Outside of Zen, however, meditation can happen in any form; sitting full lotus, half lotus, on a chair, laying down, against a wall, upside down, sideways, on your head, or walking like a crab… You do whatever position it takes for you to be in the most comfortable position you can be without the distraction of aching muscles and joints. Meditation is about taming the mind, not the body, so if we get too caught up in trying to be in the most perfect full lotus position, then we're defeating the purpose of meditation.

In my book, *Making Friends With Our Mind: A Basic Guide to Buddhist Meditation*, I think, is a great introductory to the "all-purpose" meditation methods, postures, techniques, etc.

Your body/posture has nothing to do with reaching a correct state of mind. Only your mind has something to do with reaching a correct state of mind, so once you've found your "go-to" posture, no matter what it is, then you begin your practice of reaching whatever state of mind you're trying to get to.

I'm still trying to figure out which type of meditation suits me best. Tried mindfulness, and been practicing Zazen for a while now, but I want to meditate more on the Four Noble Truths and that -meditating on a subject other than breathing- is new to me. Seems a lot harder to me because I can't really imagine how you actually meditate on a subject. As in, what do you focus on? I'm used to

124

focusing on my breath, and I can't imagine how you incorporate 'something' into it.
Like: meditate on why something is making me suffer. For instance, do you contemplate on a sentence or a specific subject? Can't figure this out…

All meditation is essentially the same; tame your mind – that is the fundamental "goal" of meditation. But just like there are different schools and traditions of Buddhism to suit different people's needs. Likewise, there are different methods of meditation. Meditating on the breath is a universal practice among all that meditate, Buddhist and non-Buddhist because it's the easiest and quickest way to focus.

However, when we meditate on "something," like suffering, etc. You're basically talking to yourself in your head, but you are doing two things: 1) You're going over what you know about the topic. In this case, suffering, you review what you know about suffering and how you understand it. 2) You're debating with yourself. Why does it make sense, why doesn't it? What is YOUR definition/understanding of suffering, etc.?

That's how we contemplate on things. We go over the subject matter with ourselves and review the lesson. Sure we can do this outside of meditation, but doing it in the quietude of meditation gives us better focus and less distraction from our surroundings.

That's basically the gist of it.

I've been practicing meditation for the last week or so and lately after every session I get really tired, and I almost fall asleep. Is that normal?

It is. I like to think that meditation for beginners is like taking a Benadryl and forcing yourself to stay awake, or getting drunk and trying to sober yourself up. Even for experienced meditators, they still feel drowsy sometimes. Heck, I still get drowsy sometimes! Well, maybe because I'm up at 5 am every morning meditating, but still.

It's really all about practice. Not just about sitting there and trying to stay awake, but practicing on your concentration. What happens when we lay on the couch when we're watching TV and not pay attention? We start to fall asleep. Likewise, if we're meditating without a focus point or an object of concentration, we're going to start dozing off.

The best way to practice this is by concentrating on your breath by counting it. Take a few deep breaths first and start counting. Breath in-out as 1, in and out again as 2, etc. up until 10 and repeat. If for some reason you've lost count or got distracted, start over again at 1 and repeat. This is a great exercise and a practice you can do for years!

I've been having trouble controlling my thoughts. I just get overwhelmed with them, and I've been trying to calm my mind. Have any tips?

"Calming our mind" does not mean controlling our thoughts. With all the controlling you're trying to do, has it helped and gotten you anywhere? No, because that's not how it works. Calming our mind means understanding our mind. We "control" our thoughts by acknowledging them, know they're there, and letting them go!

Our mind constantly wants attention; that's why it's always filled with a million thoughts ALL the time! So when a thought arises during meditation, and we start playing with it because we're trying to control it and make it go away, it plays back harder, and it's more difficult for it to actually go away.

Instead, when a thought arises, we basically say hello to it, acknowledge the thought without entertaining it (meaning, adding to it and playing out the scene) and naturally just let it go. It might feel like more thoughts arise by doing this, which will probably happen, but that's just our mind trying to get our attention.

Eventually, with LOTS of practice, our mind will get the point, and less and less thoughts will arise.

I've always had concentration problems, and I find it really difficult to stop my mind from wandering when meditating. This makes meditation really frustrating, rather than calming because I can't concentrate for more than a few seconds. I know it'll get better the more I practice it but until then, any tips, tricks or remedies that could help? Also, how are you supposed to concentrate on the present moment if the present moment is the past as soon as you think of it?

Contrary to popular belief, meditation is not just about calming our mind, which is obviously nearly impossible. Not even some of the highest ranking monks can simply sit down thoughtless and blissful; there is always a wandering thought somewhere.

So, meditating is about observing our mind. It's about watching what goes by. Just like laying outside watching the clouds go by and trying to make images out of the cloud's shapes, likewise, we just need to sit down and watch our thoughts go by and put titles to the images.

Vipassana meditation is the meditation where all we do is watch our breath, body and thoughts/feelings. For

128

every breath we take, we note to ourselves, "breathing in, breathing out" or simply counting our breath. For every movement we make with our body, we note to ourselves "moving" or "adjusting," or whatever it is we're doing. And for every thought, we note to ourselves, "thinking." Or we can be more specific, "food," "hunger," "happy," "angry," etc.

By mindfully watching everything we do while, in meditation, we're telling ourselves, "hey, I know what you're doing, and I'm watching you." The more mindful we become, especially with our thoughts, the fewer distractions will arise.

The present movement doesn't necessarily mean RIGHT NOW in this VERY millisecond of a moment. It just means being mindful and observant of yourself and your surroundings. If we regularly go outside, we might have a routine; walk the dog around the neighborhood, get coffee at a local shop, chat with some neighbors, etc. But if we sit and meditate outside and be mindful of the present moment, we might hear and realize things we've never known or noticed, like the sound and smell of the wind, birds, the rattling of a house or building, and, of course, our own body. That's what being present really means.

Part V

Suffering, Impermanence, Attachment and Self

I'm Trying To Find My Inner Peace, But I Just Can't Seem To Find It... What Would Be The Best Way To Find It?

By stop looking for it. Peace and happiness are not a destination or something we can search for externally and hang on to. We can't just go to the Happiness Store and grab some peace and happiness off the shelves! The more or harder we try to "find" peace or happiness, the further and harder it is to find.

To those new or fairly new to Buddhism or meditation might meditate for 10-15 minutes and end the session saying, "My meditation didn't work. Nothing happened!" It's because we have this false assumption that there's going to be an "aha!" moment or finish line in meditation, and guess what? There isn't one!

We can't rush things just because we want the results now. We can't skip the basics and foundations that are fundamental towards success and just skip to the end. It doesn't work like that, and we will fail, and we will lose faith and confidence and give up.

We might feel like we're making no progress, but every day when we use correct effort, we are sowing the seeds of success. So it might take a week, a month, a year or more for these seeds to ripen, but, at least, they're there, and we know the more we work at it and maintain the garden, the better the chances these seeds will grow and flourish.

If we expect to go to the gym just one time and come out looking like Arnold Schwarzenegger, and we don't, we'll think the gym or our workout isn't working and just stop! But if we apply diligent effort and have confidence in ourselves, happiness and peace will naturally come when we understand and accept the things that are not happy and peaceful.

I'm very concerned about how people judge me; sometimes it becomes a huge weight. I'm so afraid of looking stupid in front of people. I'm terrified of judgment cause anything other people say could be true, and in the worst case, it is (according to my mind). I read about emptiness and studied a bit of Buddhism. Every time I think about it I understand that it is not good to be so concerned. But

sometimes it is a feeling so strong. Could u please help me?

Show me what other people are saying? Show me the judgments or words? I want you to physically put it in my hand. You can't, right? Words are like blank bullets – they can't kill you, but they can hurt you if you're unprotected. Our protected mind is like a bullet-proof vest. It's there to stop the bullet from penetrating our body. Likewise, we train our mind to be word-proof vests to stop negative words and actions from penetrating our mind.

If I called you a purple cow, does that actually make you a purple cow? Or if I called you a giant tree or something because you're so tall, are you physically a giant made out of a tree? Absolutely not.

As unenlightened beings, we assume that we are our minds, and our minds are us, but in reality, our mind is separate from us, but because it's attached to us and we constantly listen to it, we come to the conclusion that everything we think is true. Why do we suffer? Because our mind tells us that this or that is a bad situation and that we should feel bad, depressed, sad, anxious, etc. about it and it causes us to suffer.

Truly happy people are happy because they don't allow their false judgments to take over situations and their lives. If we can't see the beauty in a chaotic world, then all we have left is suffering.

That is a major meditation practice – to meditate on the trueness of things. If you "think" people are saying things about you, sit down and meditate on those words. Meditate on the trueness and falseness of those words and break through their untrue gates. When we can start doing that for everything, we become much happier and peaceful people.

If everything is impermanent, then what is the purpose of this universe, this creation?

Not even our great and beautiful universe is permanent! It's changing, expanding, dying and creating new life. If we look up at the sky, we see millions of stars – we think of them as these big, beautiful, shining lights that are always there because society has named them and put them in constellations. But in reality, in the reality of the star, it has already died, turned into dust, created a new star, or created a black hole. So our reality is an illusion of what we think we see in the sky.

In Buddhism, there's no concept of creation or God because that doesn't matter. Buddhism isn't a God-oriented religion, it's a self and mind-oriented religion and path. So why the universe exists or why we exist as humans will probably be an unanswered question for as long as civilization exists. What we do know is that life is suffering, and we are suffering in a cycle of birth and death, and what we care about is getting out of that cycle. We are changing and dying just like the universe that also suffers death and rebirth (in its own way). We are one with the universe. We *are* the universe. We are created from substances from the universe. So when this world eventually dies and ends this form of its life, another one will be created, and the next Buddha will teach us the way to liberation.

For Buddhists, and any sentient being, our purpose in life is to be happy! To be happy and compassionate and share that with the world. In many countries and societies around the world, we can notice the happiest of people are sometimes the poorest. Why? Because they found true inner peace with their circumstances. The kind of happiness and peace that fame and fortune can never give. And this happiness they have is like a disease, because when they share their happiness and compassion towards all sentient beings, everyone around them also find happiness and compassion! Fame and fortune only give temporary happiness. It only gives us that momentary high of happiness until whatever made us happy fades away and then we want more of it. So, we go after it over and over again, always finding newer, bigger things to satisfy this thirst for temporary feelings that causes us to suffer; to become attached, addicted and greedy.

135

So be happy! Smile! Practice daily meditation and be compassionate and kind to those who treat us the worst, because they are the ones that need it most! And over time, those who were unhappy will become happy because of us and our example!.

So if you don't achieve your "outer" purpose and achieve your "inner" purpose it's ok? In other words, in the end, whatever we achieve (as in material things/goals) won't matter? At all? Want to make sure I'm understanding this right.

How could it? Or, why would it? All of the material things we accumulate and keep our whole life are just that: things. We can't take them with us when we die, so why would they matter? Not saying we can't have fancy, expensive things, or things at all, but we can't become attached to them – we don't want to be the person who loves their things so much we want to be buried with them!

All some people want are things, things, and more things! Whether it's because they're hoarders, or its because they think nice things will make them happy, popular, or up-to-date. Sure, we want the new iPhone because it's going to be amazing, but then we just have to realize it's only going to be amazing until the next iPhone is released! If there's anything in the world that's surely impermanent, it's the iPhone! Will we be getting it? Maybe eventually. But when we do, we're not going to cling to the fact that we have an iPhone. We won't be letting it distract us from finding true, inner happiness. Real happiness isn't the things we can buy or have. We're only happy with our new iPhone for as long as we have it in our hands and see it, but when we put it down, take a shower, or go to sleep, we forget about it, and the happiness we got from it is gone! Instead, we must find our true inner happiness, because that happiness *will* be with us when we sit down, take a shower, and go to sleep.

Just remember no matter how happy things might make us, until its death (it gets broken, etc.) or our own death, we can't take it with us into the next life. Instead, acknowledge and tell ourselves, "This new iPhone gives me temporary and impermanent happiness. True happiness is finding liberation and my True Buddha Nature."

I have a question in regards to a Buddha quote "we can only lose what we cling to." Does this include people, our loved ones? How would it be possible to

not cling to your husband or family pet? Isn't the
relationships we build the foundation of happiness?

If we think our husband or wife and family pet are
going to create lasting happiness, then we'll never be
truly happy. True, lasting happiness doesn't come from
external circumstances. Real happiness can only be found
within, from ourselves. What Buddha means by "we can
only lose what we cling to" is that whatever we attach to;
our family, house, car, pets, electronics, etc., will only
cause us to suffer. Why? Because none of these things
are permanent. Our significant other will grow old, get
sick, and die, and so will our pets. And when they do, are
we still happy?

Therefore, external happiness from sensual or
emotional pleasures can't really make us happy for too
long. It's *okay* to want and have things like family,
friends, pets, fancy cars and houses, and everything
above, but it's *not* okay to cling to these things as if they
will last forever and bring us lasting happiness and joy.
Look around. Everything we see will eventually age, rot,
crumble, get destroyed, and cease to exist. Our house can
last for hundreds of years, but eventually, it will start to
fall apart. Our nice car will stop running smoothly after
so many thousands and thousands of miles. Not even our
own Earth and sun will last forever.

True happiness is accepting and acknowledging that
all these things are impermanent and won't be around

forever. Once we accept and become content and mindful of life's impermanence, our losses will be much more bearable. Once we can see the true nature of all things, we will see lasting happiness.

How to reconcile between thinking and feeling? Most of the time I act based on feelings, which I have to repent later on. Even though my thoughts are clear?

Tough question. Thinking is a natural thing. Because we have perceptions, when we see, hear, touch, taste, or have feelings for something, we're going to create an idea about it. We think because of our feelings, and because of our feelings we think. Both are illusions and creations of our mind. All feelings are our own creation, whether the feeling is good, bad, attractive, or unattractive, we think that they have this independent, real quality to them, that everything we think or feel is true and right. However, this is false. If everything we think or feel causes us to believe that they are inherently true, then these thoughts and feelings would be true for everyone and everyone would think and feel the exact same way.

We might have heard the quote, "think before you speak." This is a half right, half wrong idea. Because if what we're thinking is that something is good, bad, attractive or unattractive, then we can conclude that this is something we've created and projected by our mind. However, we are not perfect beings. We are not yet highly realized or enlightened, so these mistakes will always be one of our faults. That's okay. Because once we realize this, we'll realize that our view of reality is exaggerated and one-sided.

Sometimes we commit sexual misconduct because we have feelings of lust and desire. At that time, we don't notice that we're being sucked into the trap of lust and desire until later when we feel bad and repent. Desire is one of the major causes of suffering. With ignorance and attachment, it is the source of our mistaken views and dissatisfaction. Once we train our mind to go beyond seeing things as just good or bad, attractive or unattractive, and be able to view everything with equanimity, we won't have to be controlled by our thoughts and feelings.

Can you explain the "self"?

The goal of Buddhist practice is to find our true self. This body, our form, our name, this life… is only a grain of sand in the vast ocean of our Buddha Nature. Who were we before we were John Doe? Who will we be after

John Doe? Our present form is simply a perception of our mind. Our true Self, the Buddha we will all become is hidden behind a dirty mirror.

Our mind is a mirror. We have a mirror mind. It's all fogged up like the foggy mirror after we get out of a hot shower. Behind this foggy mirror is our true Self. The fog represents our ignorance, greed, and anger – the poisons that keep us from discovering the truth. To clean this mirror we might use the wet towel we just dried off with, but the towel barely cleaned the mirror. The mirror is still foggy, and now streaky with little fuzzies from the towel. So then we try to use our hand, but still it only took away some of the fogginess and the fuzzies. Our hand cleaned it up a little bit, and we can begin to see a shape that is us. So then we use a hand towel to wipe away some more. The mirror is free of fogginess, but now it's streaky and not completely clean. Now we can, at least, see if there's any soap left in our hair. Our form is starting to look familiar but not completely clear. Finally, we use a window cleaner and a paper towel to clean off the mirror.

The mirror is now completely crystal clear, and we can see all our pores and white hairs. We've found ourselves. Likewise, to find our true self, we must work to clear the fogginess of our ignorance, greed, and anger from our mind. It takes effort and resources to clear away the fog, but in the end, the benefit is total freedom…

Liberation. Buddhism gives us the tools and resources to reach our liberation. It is our job to make the effort, determination, and motivation to use the tools and resources. Otherwise, we will always be looking at a foggy mirror; wondering who is behind it.

I am someone that feels exhausted with OCD and other desires. I constantly want more and more, and obsess on it. I realize that this pattern won't work. No matter how much you get, you'll just want more. Do you think there is no value to striving to get a glamorous career, and be what people call "successful" if in the end all you do is want more and more and never end up being satisfied? Or is there lesser value in this, we can enjoy it for a time, but it's not a central part of life?

There's no problem with wanting things, a big house, fancy car, and a successful career. The only problem is attaching to them and relying on them for our happiness. It's a natural feeling for people to want more after they've managed to get something. For example, before the iPhone, no one wanted the iPhone. When it was debuting, everyone wanted it because it was the cool, new thing. People wanted it even more when they were able to hold it, play with it and see what it could do. So because we've established this initial desire for the iPhone, every time the next version is released, we'll always want it because the perfectly functioning iPhone we have now just isn't enough.

Desire is sometimes necessary. We have to desire to become liberated, to become a Buddha. But if our desires are harmful to ourselves or others, then it's a selfish, bad desire. We have to meditate on our desires and contemplate on *why* we desire. What kind of lasting happiness do we think it'll bring us? If it's something we know we'll lose, break, or get bored of, then why even bother? Practicing generosity is a good first step to getting over our selfish desires. Giving away personal items to charity, Good Will, or to the homeless can help us break that "I want everything" bond. Slowly, but surely, our desires will lessen until we can be happy with little and look at the beauty of the world around us without all of our "things" blocking our view.

Having come from emptiness (nowhere), returning to emptiness (nowhere), why do we manifest in samsara?

Emptiness isn't exactly "nowhere." It's not nothing, zero, or empty. Emptiness simply means that the things we see every day, the people, cars, houses, plants, etc., are not really *just* people, cars, houses, plants, etc. Emptiness is almost unexplainable beyond the superficial explanation about to be given; it is something we each have to discover individually on our own, in our own way. And everyone has their own interpretation.

When we look at a flower, we automatically think "flower" or "rose" or "tulip." Looking at it from "emptiness," it isn't just a flower, but also the components that make up that flower; the soil, the sun, water, air – all these put together make the flower and then when the flower is made, we call it "flower." Our delusion and ignorance don't let us see or think of anything besides "flower."

Look around us, *nothing* is made up on its own. Nothing has come about without external causes to make that effect. A car is not a car without its engine or any of the other thousand components that allow it to run and take us from point A to point B. As humans, we are human and alive because of our organs, oxygen, and food. Not even a nail or a screw is made on its own. It's made from a machine, that needs its own parts and screws, a person to operate and put together the machine who needed parents to exist, the machine is made from metal, that needed the earth and all the elements and time to create it. Everything comes from something. Seeing that is emptiness.

So we're in this cyclic samsaric cycle because of our ignorance. Ignorance and desire are the main causes of our suffering and our obstacles that are in the way of our liberation. Because we see things and people as this "oneness," as this thing to last forever, and constantly desiring it and desiring more, that will keep us from escaping samsara. So with a disciplined meditation practice and constant learning, we can shorten the distance to the shore of enlightenment.

I've been thinking a lot about the focus on attachment being negative in Buddhism. (Recently began trying to enlighten myself/others) I've hit a bit of a rump trying to find out where this attachment being detrimental sits in my life, because of my love toward family members, as in my mother, or boyfriend. Are these feelings of extreme love wrong? Are they detrimental in my path? I feel as if I may be misinterpreting my strong love for unhealthy attachment, but I needed clarification.

Love and attachment are two very different things. Love is necessary for our and others' happiness. Attachment is the greediness we have that assumes we need what we want/love.

It's absolutely fine to love, especially our loved ones. However, what makes this love "dangerous" or prone to attachment is our ignorance and lack of understanding of impermanence. We always make assumptions and hopes that our family will out-live anyone else, or that when we think we've found our soul mate that they'll be around forever and never leave you. But in reality, our parents will grow old, get sick and die. Our soul mate might be our soul mate for 10, 20 or 30 years, but feelings and love changes, and the relationship might end. What happens at the end of all these examples? Hurt. Sadness. Depression. Anger. Hate.

As Buddhists, our main goal is to lessen and eradicate our attachments. It doesn't have to be by getting rid of stuff/people. We don't have to give away all our clothes, belongings, money, or stop seeing and talking to family and friends. No, no. It's much simpler than that. We simply have to meditate on these things and reflect on them; visualize your things burning, getting lost, stop working, etc. and visualize on death, of your friends and family. After much practice, we'll come to a powerful realization that everything is impermanent – everything will come to an end. It's inevitable.

Why do we practice meditation on death and the end of things? Because when it does happen, our understanding of its end will be so much easier to live with. If we don't want to hurt so much, have anger and

maybe even hate when a loved one dies, then it's
important to meditate on death, so when the time comes,
it's an easier process for you and those around you.

***What are your thoughts on the Law of Attraction?
I've done some research and noticed that it
primarily focuses on Positive thinking and
attracting the things you want in your life, instead
of negative things. It seems as if it's a change in
attitude and how you see things. It's tricky because
it also states that you must Ask(Fully know what
you want), Believe (Have faith that you will get it)
and Receive (Act as if you already have it and be
thankful). What would you say about this?***

I would say that it sounds a lot like a Buddhist
teaching! Sorta. Buddhism is a mind-centered practice,
right? So our objective in life is to seek and find
happiness from within instead of external circumstances.
We all know that one person who is always happy,
energetic, positive and just loves everything about life –
what's the difference between them and most people?
They see the beauty in life even when they are
surrounded by chaos and disappointment.

For example, if you allowed someone to verbally
hurt you (they called you names or talked behind your

back) or if you didn't get your dream job that you for
sure thought you had, will sobbing, hating and being
angry help you or anyone else around you? No! If
someone called you an ugly horse, does that
actually make you an ugly horse? Last time I checked,
horses can't get on the Internet and ask questions! It's all
about your attitude and the way you choose to look at and
react to things.

I'm not saying that positively thinking about
winning the lottery is going to make you win the lottery,
but it will help you cope with the inevitable loss. We all
have this intrinsic value, this Buddha Nature, though we
can't see it yet, we have to believe that it's there because
we're all bound to become Buddhas eventually. We
practice Buddhism because we want to become a
Buddha, we have that faith in ourselves that if we
practice this moral and good life, our good actions will
bring us good results.

Instead of the "law of attraction," in Buddhism, it
would be the "law of the state of the mind." With a
positive mind, a positive outlook on life is seen and when
bad things happen, it isn't seen as bad, but simply life
walking its course.

Could you please explain the Buddhist concept of getting rid of Ego (which I understand to be our sense-of-self)? And also, I don't understand how it would be beneficial for people to get rid of that. It seems that without the ego, anything that makes us unique is dissolved. A well-developed sense of identity is considered a healthy part of development in modern psychology, so how would Buddhism address that position?

There's a difference between ego and personality. Personality is what makes who we are: our likes and dislikes, our humor and boringness, our identity. Our ego is our wants, needs, and desires. Neither of the two is the real us. We are not our personality and ego; we think we are because it controls us – it tells us what we want to eat, wear, say, do and go.

The personality is a temporary phenomenon that we cling to because it's what we and others know our identity to be. But once we become more aware of our trueness, of our aliveness, without the mask of our name and body, then we can see what we truly are.

Even modern psychology will say that our personality and ego has been created and is dependent on our environment and culture. If we grew up and lived in the fanciest of Beverly Hills or Hollywood with all that we've ever wanted without a single moment of suffering, would our personality, ego and mentality be the same if we were to grow up and live in Texas on a farm doing farm work? Of course not!

Our personality and ego are temporary, it can change, but our true selves is the real "us" and moves with us from life to life until it reaches enlightenment.

How can you let go of such things like anger or pride? I have such a hard time becoming unattached and could really use help.

I don't think we can truly let go of *all* anger. Both the Dalai Lama and Thich Nhat Hanh, the most peaceful people I have ever seen, have admitted that they have moments of anger. I always try to stay positive, happy and all tree-huggery whenever I can. Until I drive… then I hate everyone on the road! That's where my pride bites me in the butt, because I'm assuming I'm a better driver than all the grandmas on the road and that I'd be one heck of a Nascar driver!

But… mindfulness brings me back to reality and reminds me that, no, people aren't slow, bad drivers, they're just following the speed limit. And no, I probably won't be a Nascar driver, because I'd probably kill myself just trying to get into one of those crazy cars!

Things such as anger, jealousy, pride, etc., are all "fake," made up feelings created by our own mind. These feelings aren't real, we can't see it, touch it, smell it, taste it – they are things we made up to make sense of situations that are happening to us. Why did you get angry? Because someone called you fat and stupid? Unless you're actually fat and stupid, someone calling you that doesn't actually make you fat and stupid. Instead, you allowed yourself to make what they said real when it was simply just empty words that you could have just laughed at and let go.

And then there's our pride. Our beautiful egotistical voice in our head that tells us that we're just so much better than everyone else. But are we really? No. If we were, we wouldn't be asking questions. In moments where we constantly compare ourselves to others, we're failing to challenge ourselves to our fullest potential. There is no such thing as being number one. How many World Records are constantly being broken? Hundreds, thousands! Why? Because, there is always someone better!

You think you're the best at your job? You're not. There is someone that is more educated and more experienced that could make you look like a secretary. Yet, our pride is always there telling us we're better than everyone else. The result? Ignorance. Jealousy. Anger. Wrong view. Wrong path. So it's important to be mindful as much as we can, so we can remind ourselves to stay grounded in any situation.

Of course, meditation helps. Meditate on the Four Immeasurables (Compassion, loving-kindness, appreciative joy, and equanimity). The Immeasurables will, hopefully, remind you to stay grounded, mindful and present.

How would you go through the process of letting go of ego? And bringing the true self to the surface. I've been suffering with this for a while.

Practice! Our ego is the failure and success of our lives. It creates and feeds our desires and greed, which ultimately leads us to suffering (dissatisfaction). To eradicate ego, we practice non-attachment to things, people and ideas. We must let go of the idea that we're somehow the best of the best, the highest, most honored one of all… Well, we're not. Not even close. Not even the President has that status. Presidents become Presidents because they have the money to fulfill a campaign and win people over, but there are dozens of other people who can't afford a campaign that would probably be much better at the job. So we must remember there is always, always someone better than us.

Then we must detach from our ideas of self and others, rid the opinions and stereotypes of a certain group of people or things. We're all entitled to our opinions, but it must be an opinion based on wisdom, not mere superficial observance.

Meditate on yourself. Cultivate compassion for yourself. Come to a realization that this body, this name, and personality is not truly you. Your body is only a new vessel of a new life. Your name is only a title your parents gave you to distinguish you from others. Your personality is something that grows and changes according to your environment. Nothing is truly real and permanent, so we must overcome that notion. Meditation is key and must be practiced diligently with self-discipline.

Part VI

Karma, Rebirth and Dying

What Do You Think Would Be A Good Way To Explain Death To A Child, From A Buddhist Perspective?

Buy a plant or flowers, if possible that you can plant or put in the garden. Let the child care for it, water it, etc. Let them witness it flourishing and dying and re-flourishing again when the seasons come back. This is a great way to explain to them that life, in any form, will be born, get old, get sick, die and then come back again when it's ready. That all life goes from one form to another, even us.

Of course, maybe they'll ask, where was I before or where will I go afterward. Even adults ask these questions, but the answer is always, "You will find them." As they get older and can meditate with you and you help explain to them meditation and its practices, they will be able to contemplate and develop the wisdom to find their true nature – the being that is not past,

155

present or future – the real purpose that takes us from one life to another.

This form, this body is only a vessel. A hotel that we check in while traveling for business. Here, the hotel represents our body and the person checking in (the businessperson) is our consciousness. Each trip the business person checks in from one hotel to another, traveling everywhere, doing business, trying to be successful. Likewise, we go from one form of life to another trying to find ways to be successful, successful at realizing enlightenment.

As we go from one hotel to another, until we reach our final destination and get out of the hotel jumping game, we get to enjoy our success and fortune. So death is a natural and necessary part of life. Even if we realized enlightenment in this lifetime, we still have to die, but we die knowing that we will not be reborn (unless we choose to) into a life of suffering.

Would our next rebirth be influenced by Buddhist changes we have made in this life? For example, if we did not achieve enlightenment but we began the journey, would this be erased from our consciousness in our next life, until we begin all over again?

A simple answer: No. We are where we are today because of the karma of our past lives. And it's our karma in this life that determines how good or bad our next life will be. Until we become Enlightened, our present and all our future lives will share, use, gain, and lose the same good or bad karma.

Because we're on a Buddhist path now, we're already gaining good karma. We're earning "points," or merit, for a better future life, and several lives after that. However, although we take with us the karma that has been accumulated in past lives into our future lives, any realization we've made in one life will have to be re-realized in the next. Although with each life, that realization will come easier and easier.

In Buddhism, the belief is that we have eight consciousnesses. Our eighth consciousness, referred to as the "store-house consciousness," is where all our experiences, our good and bad seeds, are stored and brought back up again in future lives. So all the good or bad deeds that we do, or any positive or negative seeds that we sow will go to and come from our store consciousness. So the quality of our future lives is determined by our eighth consciousness.

***If I don't know what wrong karma I did in my
previous lives then how can I correct my karma in
my present life? Is there a way to understand past
karmas in present lives?***

Not really. Until we've realized Enlightenment, we
can't "see" our past lives. Past karma isn't really as
important as our present karma. We should be more
worried about our present and future karma/life than our
past because there's nothing we can do about it.

However, we can create a fairly general idea of any
good/bad karma from our past lives in our present life.
Are we poor, comfortable, rich? Good looking, average,
not good looking? Do we do well in academics, hobbies,
or extracurricular activities? Are we better at something
than something else? Do we have an odd talent or no
talent? We can judge our present life and give a general
assumption if past lives have done good or bad to create
our good or bad present life. So even though we might
not know our next life, it's important to better it in this
life. All our good and bad deeds/karma will affect us –
either in this life, the next, or any future lives. So if we're
practicing Buddhism, or just practicing a virtuous, good
life, be happy to know that our next life will be much
better, happier, healthier and longer.

I have accumulated much debt. I have always had a non-material outlook, but recently it has intensified. I am considering defaulting on some loans, letting my car go back, etc. I know I signed a contract. I'm reaping the karma of my actions; I am a slave to debt. If I stop paying my bills, how would this be viewed in Buddhist context?

As humans, we're always going to be a slave to debt, whether it's to the bank, family, friends, or co-workers. We're even in debt to the people (farmers) who provide us food. Debt is going to follow us until the day we die. We can run away and live in a cave in China and never have to worry about paying any of our debt back, but what we will be paying back is our karmic debt. Just because *we* got away from our debt in this life, doesn't mean the *debt* is gone too.

Even in future lives, in some way, shape, or form we still have to owe that debt. This is why monastics are required to be debt-free upon ordaining – and also so the government won't come after them for abandoning debt. The best thing we can do is just to stop accumulating more debt and work on paying things off.

Unless we win the lottery, there's really nothing we can do except work on paying it off as much as we comfortably can. And of course, stop adding on unnecessary debt. Sometimes we have to make sacrifices to do it, like getting a cheaper car, or a smaller house or apartment, and not having all the pretty things we want.

Along with monetary debt, paying back a karma debt could also mean paying back a life (usually ours, but could also be loved ones). There's a story (and this is roughly how it's remembered) of a virtuous monk whom in a past life killed someone. He was a great king's personal monk (teacher). The monk knew he was on the verge of Enlightenment, but before he could, he had to pay a debt. One day during a Dharma teaching to the king, a raging man came running towards the monk with a sword attempting to slash at the monk. The king's guards quickly stopped the man from reaching the monk. But the monk knew why he was there and what he was going to do, so he asked the king to let the man go and continue his mission. So the man was let loose and killed the monk. This was the monk's final debt to end his cycle in Samsara.

So being debt-free is also required to be freed from Samsara because we still have that attachment. Though this attachment is unwanted, nonetheless, it's still an attachment that we need to release in order to find liberation. So again, as much and as comfortably as we can, we need to try to pay off our debts – financial and karmic debts. Not only will it be beneficial for our karma, it'll also just give us a much more sense of freedom!

I was wondering if, in a theoretical situation, someone found an animal in pain, dying and was suffering badly; would it be against Buddhism to put the animal out of it's severe suffering by killing it? (As painlessly as possible that is).

It is *very* situational. In circumstances if there is absolutely anything we can do to save a living being, then we must do it. For practitioners who take the Bodhisattvas Vows, sometimes that means risking their own life to save others. But then there are situations where there is truly nothing else we can do. Though our intentions are good, we will still be affected by negative karma, though on the lesser side based on our helpful intentions.

At my temple, we have a "mini temple," basically, a meditation room in the garden that at one point or another gets a hornets nest or two inside. Because it's a "popular" spot for meditators and visitors, someone eventually has to go in there to remove the nests and spray down the room to kill anything else in hiding for the sake of the safety of others.

When and if in a situation where killing is needed, a mercy kill, it's important to have the right intention and do everything we can first before taking life. Then, if having to take life, it's also important to pray for the being. For example, when I'm in this situation, I will pray: "I'm sorry. May you be reborn in a better life.

Namo Amitabha Buddha. Namo Amitabha Buddha.
Namo Amitabha Buddha…" repeating Amitabha's name
ten times.

Does destiny exist? And what is the real meaning of this world? Because if karma exist then destiny also exists… Could you please explain what is your thought on this topic?

Karma and destiny are two very different things.
There is no "destiny" in Buddhism because that would
mean our lives and our futures are fixed and cannot be
changed. That is completely incorrect. Karma is not
fixed. Our lives and our future can change with our own
efforts and actions.

If "destiny" said your life was meant for failure, all
you have to do is flip destiny off and go to college! Get a
good degree with a good job and your life is changed for
success and opportunity. No one or thing can tell you
what you can or cannot do, or how you should or
shouldn't live. Even the Buddha told his disciples, "Out
of respect for me because I am the Buddha, do not take
what I say as truth. Instead, take it and apply it to your
life – experiment with what works and doesn't work for
you."

Part VII

Numbers, Steps and Lists

What's Special About The Number 108?

According to Buddhism, it is said that people have 108 afflictions or kleshas. The six senses (sight, sound, taste, touch, smell, and consciousness) multiplied by three reactions (positive, negative and indifferent), making 18 "feelings."

Each of these feelings can be either "attached to pleasure" or "detached from pleasure," making 36 "passions" each of which may be manifested in the past, present or future. All the combination of these things makes a total of 108.

What are the Six Perfections?

The Six Paramitas (Perfections) are a guide for the Mahayana Buddhist. They are virtues to be cultivated to strengthen our practice and bring us to enlightenment. The paramitas describe the True Nature of an enlightened being, which is to say they are our own true nature. We can also say we are all essentially enlightened beings, but we are clouded by the three poisons: ignorance, greed and anger.

Our true nature is like the person behind the foggy mirror after we take a hot shower. At first, we forget or don't realize the mirror is foggy because we go about our routine without looking into the mirror. But then when we want the mirror, when we want to see ourselves, we use the towel, a cloth or our hands to wipe away the fog, trying to clean it off. We use different methods to clean it off, but leaving behind traces of the towel, cloth or streaks. But as we continue to clean the mirror, we get closer and closer to seeing ourselves.

Likewise, when we cultivate these paramitas, we bring this true nature into expression, and we start perfecting ourselves to become true bodhisattvas. So the Six Paramitas are:

1. Generosity (Dana)
2. Morality (Sila)
3. Patience (Ksanti)
4. Energy (Virya)
5. Meditation (Dhyana)
6. Wisdom (Prajna)

1.   Generosity (Dana)

The perfection of generosity is true generosity of spirit. It is giving from a sincere desire to benefit and help others, without the expectation of a reward or recognition. There must be no selfishness attached. Even when doing charity or volunteer work to "feel good about ourselves" is not true generosity. If our intention is not absolutely in the mindset of truly wanting to benefit others or doing something because we were asked or felt like we had to say yes, it is not true generosity.

If we see an old lady needing help with her groceries, and we think, "Maybe I should help her," then that is not of true generosity. True generosity is when our help or benefit to others comes automatically, without having to think about it or of the benefits or reward of helping. Generosity doesn't just mean giving material or physical help; it also means giving spiritual help or helping people with their fear of aging, getting sick and dying. And giving loving-kindness and compassion to all beings.

2.   Morality (Sila)

Morality, or discipline, in Buddhism, doesn't mean obediently following a list of rules. Of course, Buddhism has many lists, that's how we remember and learn things, and one of the most important lists is our precepts. But the precepts are more like a guide instead of a strict set of rules. An enlightened being responds to any situation correctly without having to refer to a set of rules. But we accept and take these precept vows so we can refrain from doing negative actions and cultivate compassion and help others.

3.   Patience (Ksanti)

The translation of Ksanti literally means "able to withstand." There are three characteristics to patience:

1) <u>Enduring personal hardships:</u> cultivating with this aspect of patience begins with accepting the first Noble Truth; that life is suffering, that life is dissatisfying. We accept that life is difficult and full of chaos as well as being temporary. As we learn to accept suffering, we realize how much time and energy we've wasted trying to avoid the inevitable. Our biggest reaction to suffering is self-protection. We want to avoid things we don't like or want to do, or that will hurt like going to the doctor or dentist. But then we think of ourselves as unfortunate when pain does come. This reaction comes from the belief that there is a permanent "self" to protect, that we have to do everything to protect ourselves from suffering. But the more we try to avoid suffering, the more suffering we actually endure! When we realize there's nothing to protect, our perception of pain changes.

2) <u>Patience with others:</u> means not allowing others' negativity to affect us. I'm sure we've all been in

situations where others might have said or did something to upset or frustrate us, but how we handle it depends on our patience and understanding that no one can affect us but ourselves. Only when we allow or believe things will it affect us.

3) <u>Accepting truth:</u> it was already mentioned that patience begins with accepting suffering, but that also includes accepting the truth about other things like that we are angry, ignorant, greedy, jealous, and that ultimately we are responsible for our own unhappiness. Sometimes we'll read or hear great teachers say that when people are getting closer to enlightenment, they may experience great fear. This is our ego trying to preserve itself. Getting beyond that fear is a challenge.

When the Buddha was sitting in meditation the night before his Enlightenment and Mara visited him, Mara did everything in his power to distract the Buddha with anger, fear and temptation. But none of that worked because the Buddha was patient with himself and knew he was so close to his great realization. When he got beyond that, nirvana!

Also, we must accept uncertainty. For a long time, we won't see clearly. We won't have all the answers. We may never have all the answers. To walk the Buddhist path, we have to be willing not to know—to have patience and confidence in ourselves.

167

4. Energy (Virya)

Also translated as enthusiastic effort or zeal, energy means we must have the energy and effort to realize enlightenment. Energy refers to both mental and physical energy. Taking care of our body and health is part of this paramita, but for many of us, the mental energy is a bigger challenge. A lot of people struggle to make time for daily practice. Meditation or chanting might feel like the last thing we want to do sometimes, but we need to develop energy to have the motivation to practice.

The perfection of energy has three components:

1) The development of character: is about cultivating the courage and the will to walk the path as far as it goes, for as long as it takes. For most, this means correcting bad habits or giving up excuses, or both. We may need to clarify our own commitment to the path and cultivate self-trust, confidence, and conviction.

2) Spiritual training: this, of course, means learning the Dharma, the Buddha's teachings, but it could also include learning the rituals and why we do them. A clear understanding of what the Buddha taught will help our confidence and give our practice more focus. But it's not just about reading and trying to understand the teachings, it's about actively applying those teachings to our lives and practicing them.

3) Benefiting others: now it's time to help others from what we've learned. The development of bodhicitta,

the altruistic wish or desire to realize enlightenment for the benefit of all beings, is essential to Mahayana Buddhism. Bodhicitta helps us release selfish attachment to our efforts. When bodhicitta is strong, it fuels our determination to practice.

5.   Meditation (Dhyana)

Buddhist meditation, or concentration, is more popular in the West than Buddhism itself, unfortunately. Another word for concentration is Samadhi, which more specifically means one-pointed concentration. In the West, meditation is used at a therapeutic level to relieve stress, anxiety and treat behavioral disorders. But Buddhist meditation is a discipline, not a treatment. The Buddha sat in meditation for years to realize enlightenment, not because he had a headache he wanted to get rid of!

The order of the paramitas is not random. Meditative concentration comes before the last paramita, wisdom because wisdom is developed from concentration. For most, this is a gradual process. Though one may experience bliss, someone else may experience frustration, sleepiness, boredom, pain, etc. That doesn't mean we're doing it wrong, but that's just the way it is for some. So we need to be diligent with our practice to develop and succeed.

There are two main forms of meditation. *Samatha* and *Vipassana*, or in English, concentration and contemplation. Samatha means tranquility and leads to Samadhi, one-pointedness concentration. So we go from meditating and acknowledging our thoughts and feelings, to concentrating on just one thing, which is usually our breath.

Vipassana means "insight." There are a few approaches to insight meditation, but generally, we take a teaching, thought or perspective and contemplate on it to alter our basic mental orientation. We take a teaching, the first Noble Truth for example, and we contemplate on it, dissect it and learn its true meaning, our own meaning of what it teaches.

6. Wisdom (Prajna)

In Mahayana Buddhism, wisdom is the direct and ultimate realization of *Sunyata* or emptiness. Very simply, this is the teaching that all phenomena are without a self or self-essence. All phenomena without self may not sound that complicated, but as we work with prajna teaching, the significance of emptiness becomes more and more evident, and the importance of emptiness in Mahayana Buddhism cannot be overstated.

However, this wisdom can't be understood by intellect alone. We use the help of the other paramitas.

It's said that the perfection of wisdom contains all the other perfections and without it, no perfection is possible. Wisdom in this case specifically refers to emptiness. This realization is said to be the door of enlightenment.

For example, if we were to take apart this computer or smartphone, at what point does it cease to be a computer? This is a subjective judgment. Does it stop being a computer once it can't function as a computer, or does it stop being a computer when it's all in pieces? Some will say once it stops turning on it's no longer a computer. Others will say until it's broken into pieces; then it stops being a computer.

The point is, the "computer" is just a name or designation we give to a phenomena; there is no inherent "computer nature" dwelling in the computer.

There is a famous Indian monk named Nagarjuna[30] that said it is incorrect to say that things exist, but it is also incorrect to say that things don't exist. Because all phenomena exist interdependently and are void of self, and all distinctions we make between this and that phenomena are relative. So things and beings "exist" only in a relative way.

---

[30] Nagarjuna is considered one of the most important Buddhist philosophers and the founder of the Madhyamaka school of Mahayana Buddhism. He is also credited with developing the Prajnaparamita Sutras.

What are the Five Precepts?

In Buddhism, the five precepts are guidelines for moral and mindful living. They aren't necessarily rules in the sense that if we break them, we'll be punished. Instead, they are suggestions to a better way of life.

People who wish to convert and become Buddhists will take the Three Refuges[31] and Five Precepts Vows. This is a person's commitment and dedication to a better life, and to help themselves in order to help the other people. This ceremony is traditionally taken at a temple. Most temples have official dates (once or twice a year) when members will be able to participate in the ceremony.

For lay practitioners, the five precepts are presented for us to accept and uphold. However, depending if the temple will allow this or not, we can deny the last precept (abstaining from intoxicants). So the first four are mandatory. The precepts are clear and straightforward, so it's our own responsibility to use our intelligence to apply them and live by them as best we can. The five precepts are:

1. To abstain from killing/taking life
2. To abstain from stealing

---

[31] The Three Refuges, or the Triple Gem are the Buddha, the Dharma, and the Sangha.

3.   To abstain from sexual misconduct
4.   To abstain from lying
5.   To abstain from intoxicants (drugs and alcohol)

No killing, no stealing, no sexual misconduct, no lying, and no intoxicants. These suggestions are anywhere from impossible of doing. As long as we're mindful of what we do, where we step (to not step on any visible bugs) and our environment, we can abstain from killing. Being mindful and not taking what is not ours without permission, and taking office supplies from the office (or anywhere else), we can abstain from stealing.

Sexual misconduct is often confusing for some. It doesn't mean no sex; it just means to have the good kind of sex with your one spouse or partner. Having multiple partners, cheating, or having sex with someone who has a partner, is breaking this precept. Basically, if it harms anyone, their relationship or lives, it's sexual misconduct.

Abstaining from lying also includes pretending to know something we don't, exaggerating a lie, and spreading rumors. The final precept, abstaining from intoxicants, which means abstaining from alcohol and drugs, or anything that might cause "headlessness." Because we must be mindful of anything and everything we do, being drunk or high means we won't be mindful of the actions we do.

What are the do's and don'ts when visiting a Buddhist temple?

It's always important no matter what religious place we go to, to always be respectful, whether we're a religious or spiritual person or not. Many temples will have a sign or brochure that has some "Temple etiquette" rules. If not, here are some general do's and don't's:

DO'S:
- Take off your shoes before entering the Temple.
- Bow when entering the Temple.
- Bow when monks/nuns walk into the room.
- Wear respectable clothing (no beach-ware) – wearing pants or shorts below the knee is ideal, or skirts for the ladies.
- If taking pictures with a statue, keep your head below the statue's head – being on one knee is respectable.
- Keep quiet.
- When getting up during meditation or service, stand up while bowing until you're somewhat distant from the center of everything/everyone.
- Address the monk(s)/nun(s) as "Venerable," unless you know exactly how the Sangha addresses them.

DON'TS:

- Point at Buddha statues, monks, or nuns, *especially* with your feet.
- Wear "beach clothes," including tank tops and revealing clothing.
- ABSOLUTELY NO touching of the monks, nuns, or the heads of statues.
- Be loud.
- Show any public displays of affection.
- Bring kids if they don't know how to behave.
- Wear heavy perfume or cologne.
- Be chatty with monks/nuns.
- Disrupt, including taking pictures of ceremonies, events, or meditation sessions.
- Spit.
- Litter.
- Place texts or prayer sheets directly on the floor.

What are the Five Faults and Eight Antidotes?

In Tibetan Buddhism, the Five Faults (*ādīnava*) are factors in Samatha (calmness and stillness of the mind) meditation. The Five Faults identify obstacles in the meditation practice, and the Eight Antidotes are applied to overcome these obstacles. Though mainly a Vajrayana practice, these still apply to everyone's meditation practice and would be helpful to everyone to know, use, and overcome.

The Five Faults to be relinquished are:

1)   Laziness (Kausīdya): not wishing to cultivate meditative stabilization.

There are three types of laziness:

1. Laziness of not wanting to do anything

2. Laziness of discouragement (or feeling ourselves unworthy)

3. Laziness of being busy with worldly things.

2) Forgetfulness (A*vavādasammosa*): not remembering the object of meditation or a lack of mindfulness on how to do meditation properly.

3) Lethargy (or agitation: A*uddhatya)* and excitement (or dullness: *Laya*): interruptions of meditative stabilization.

4) Non-application (A*nabhisamskāra)* of the antidotes: occurring when lethargy and excitement arise.

5) Over-application (A*bhisamskāra)* of the antidotes: continuing to apply the antidotes even though lethargy and excitement have been extinguished.

The Eight Antidotes to the Five Faults are:
The antidotes to laziness are:

1) Faith (*śraddhā*): seeing the good qualities of meditative stabilization.

2) Aspiration (*chanda*): seeking to attain those good qualities.

3) Effort (*vyayama*): delighting in engaging in meditative stabilization.

4) Physical and mental pliancy (*praśrabdhi*): an effect (of effort).

The antidote to forgetfulness is:

5) Mindfulness: maintaining concentration on an object continuously.

The antidote to lethargy and excitement is:

6) Awareness: knowing that lethargy or excitement has arisen or is arising.

The antidote to non-application is:

7) Application: engaging in the antidotes to lethargy and excitement.

The antidote to over-application is:

8) Desisting from application: relaxing one's effort.

What are the Nine Levels of Meditation?[32]

The Nine Levels of Meditation, or the Nine Stages of Training the Mind, is an ancient and essential teaching on

---

[32] From the author's book: *Making Friends With Our Mind: A Basic Guide to Buddhist Meditation.*

the development of meditative concentration, also called
Samatha[33].

This teaching outlines nine basic states of
consciousness, which equate to nine qualities of
concentrated attention. We can learn how to improve our
meditation practice by comparing our own experience
with the states described here. It is important to have
confidence, vigilance, and a strong aspiration to succeed
and advance from one level to the next. Sometimes we
might get stuck on one level because we're in a state of
mind that is peaceful and comfortable. However, it's
crucial that we continue and push ourselves to succeed to
the higher levels of meditation to truly penetrate our
mind to find Truth and liberation.

Moving from one level to a superior one is achieved
by overcoming the obstacles present at each stage like
pleasure and attachment to the meditative feelings of
peace and joy. This is precisely the value of this
teaching; it allows us to immediately discover how our
practice is developing and what we need to do to advance
it.

Concentration practice (samatha) is the basis from
which we can retrieve information (insight) into the true
nature of things and reality. Therefore, concentration
practice is the ground from which the seed of meditation

---

[33] Samatha is the quiet, calmness and tranquility of the mind.

sprouts. However, concentration practice itself is not meditation. Meditation begins once concentration has been established. Actual meditation is defined as a state of consciousness within which we can retrieve insight. The first three stages – placing the mind, continuous placement, and replacing the mind – are the preparations for meditation or developing the stability needed for meditation. Stages four through seven – close placement, tamed mind, pacified mind, and complete pacification – is the actual meditation of developing a clear mind. Finally, stages eight and nine – single-pointedness and balanced placement – are building and increasing meditation strength.

1. Placing or Setting the Mind: At the first stage, we are barely able to hold onto the object of meditation before losing it. We can begin to set the mind on the object of meditation but cannot hold it for too long. We will have to bring back the object again and again and take hold of it. Because wandering thoughts are being identified with mindfulness, it may appear that there is more conceptuality than usual. These wandering thoughts appear more frequently than the object of meditation. At this stage, we recognize and experience the many distracting thoughts as they arise.

We must acknowledge that we want to keep our concentration on the object of meditation and not on concepts, thoughts, and emotions. We can mentally say, "I am focusing my mind on my breath (or whatever our object of meditation is)." Our placement strengthens when we are able to recognize a thought and return back to our object of meditation. Every time we are able to recognize a thought and go back to our object, we are moving forward by just letting thoughts go and not engaging with them. The first level is simply being able to ignore interacting with distracting thoughts and being mindful enough to go back to our object of meditation.

2. Continuous Placement: We are able to remain focused on the object of meditation for at least a few minutes. Conceptuality is beginning to lessen, and some of the mental distractions are pacified, and others appear to slow down a little and become exhausted. We are able to have continuous placement because we have confidence in the benefits of meditation. At this point, we are able to place our mind on our object of meditation for 108 cycles of the breath (one Mala round). Though we might experience some distraction, the distractions or thoughts aren't large enough to take us away from our concentration. At this stage, our mindfulness can only last for so long, and our mind will eventually drift off and forget about our object. Once our practice on our concentration reaches 108 breaths (give or take some), we are neither completely still nor completely distracted and so we have completed the second stage and can move on to the third.

3. Replacement or Resetting the Mind: We are familiar with the object we are concentrating on to the point where we can re-establish our focus on it immediately after losing it, and we no longer need to seek it. We are still bothered by some distractions and wandering thoughts, except we can quickly return to the object of meditation; we patch up the broken concentration with mindfulness. By practicing bringing back our concentration, we start to do it less and less, and our mindfulness is maturing into stability. By the end of this stage, we've reached a milestone of our concentration meditation: stability.

By now our meditation feels good and peaceful because of the stability of our mind, but it isn't as strong and clear as it could be. This stage is still a major accomplishment, though. Like a cat that's being sneaky to catch a mouse, it moves from one corner to another to get closer to the mouse, but it never loses sight of it. Similarly, our minds might move around a little, but never too far from our object of meditation.

4. Close Placement or Setting the Mind: This point is reached through the force of intense mindfulness where we can hold onto the object of meditation to the end of the session without ever breaking the continuity of our concentration. The object of meditation and focus will not be lost at this level. We can begin to apply the power of discriminating awareness.

Towards the end of the third stage and into the beginning of the fourth stage, we are dealing with obstacles such as euphoria, which becomes distracting. Using discriminating awareness, we realize this. However, by having such feelings, it gives us the hint of we still need to continue and progress with our practice. It is during this stage that we are warned about thinking that we have become highly realized or enlightened because the mind feels strong and stable, but we are not highly realized nor enlightened. We must progress and advance. If we enjoy this stability too much, our mind will become too relaxed, and we might not be able to reach the other stages. Our mind is stable, but not yet clear. The cat can't catch the mouse; it can only move around it. Likewise, we need to hone our awareness and strengthen our mind even more.

5. Tamed or Disciplined Mind: At this level, it is necessary to revivify or heighten the mind to overcome subtle sinking or weak concentration. We generate the power of contemplation and through our own power know the good qualities of meditation, so we strengthen our meditation by bringing in more clarity. Our mind is now workable. Here we never lose sight of the object of meditation, and our attention is sharp and focused. Our mind is still not completely still. Distractions and wandering thoughts still arise, but it cannot take us away from the object of meditation. Yet now, excitement again poses a threat.

Because we know the benefits and merits we can achieve through meditation by having faith, devotion, and confidence in our practice, we can become successful in focusing and taming our mind. We will be able to focus much more easily. By the end of this stage, we must be able to control our five senses (eyes, ears, nose, tongue, touch). Meaning, when one of our senses gets caught in a distraction like hearing a car alarm go off or smelling food being cooked, we have to remind ourselves to not be pulled into that distraction and to continue with our focus.

6. Pacified Mind: Reaching this stage is a victory. We feel tranquility and clarity. We are still working with a mind that is still sometimes strong and tight, and sometimes weak and loose, so our practice still needs some adjustments and effort. Meditation is improved through knowledge of the faults of various obstacles, such as being distracted by a wandering thought but still maintaining the object of meditation without it being lost. Due to the heightened awareness of our mind, there is danger of subtle excitement and laxity. To advance, we simply need to more quickly address the distractions by means of vigilance.

7. Complete Pacification: The battle of taming our mind is over, but there are still some subtle wandering thoughts about the pleasure of meditation hanging around. We might feel a little attached with how good meditation feels; tranquil and joyous. In level four we actively got rid of wandering thoughts, but in this level, we persuade them because they are like ice melting in a pit of fire. Our meditation is becoming so strong that when wandering thoughts and feelings arise, like the ice they naturally melt away. The waterfall of thoughts we had when we first sat down and started our meditation has become a calm lake with only a few ripples.

8. Single-Pointedness: Very little effort is required to remain focused upon the object of meditation for the entire session without experiencing even the slightest interruption to concentration. However, an effort is still required in the beginning of meditation to concentrate and focus on our object of meditation. We can attain and advance to the next level by the power of continuous effort. By the end of this level, those few ripples we had on our lake in level eight are now completely still.

9. Balanced Placement: At this level we are able to place the mind on the object of meditation with equanimity. Without effort, we are able to maintain perfect concentration, and our meditation has come to perfection. The mind is tame and empty of thoughts as we sit in union with the present moment. This does not mean that the ego is eliminated; it only means that the mind has settled into its natural state. This is not enlightenment; it is merely a foundation from which insight into the truth can be acquired. Our mind is centered, stable, clear, joyous, and confident. We now have a mind that is able to focus on any endeavor. Our lake-mind has now become frozen; completely still and unshakable by any subtle touch or distractions.

What are the ten levels of a Bodhisattva?

The ten levels of the Bodhisattva (*Ten Bodhisattva Bhumis*) are the stages to the path of enlightenment. Each stage represents a level of attainment and serves as a basis for the next level. Each level marks a definite advancement in one's training that is accompanied by progressively greater power.

There are Five Paths on which a Bodhisattva develops in succession. The ten levels are subcategories of the Five Paths:

1. The path of accumulation or equipment (Sambharamarga): The aspiring Bodhisattva possess a strong desire of developing Bodhicitta. When Bodhicitta is fully developed, the Bodhisattva has completely obtained Sambharamarga.

2. The path of training (Prayogamarga): The Bodhisattva meditates on emptiness until it becomes clear to them, once it does, the Bodhisattva has obtained Prayogamarga.

3. The path of seeing (Darshanamarga): After deep meditation, the Bodhisattva feels that their mind and emptiness are one and realizes the emptiness of reality. At the stage, the Bodhisattva does not create new karma but still has old karma that gets eradicated with their increasing powers.

4. The path of intense contemplation/meditation (Bhavanamarga): At this stage, the Bodhisattva has purified themselves of past karma and defilements and accumulates wisdom.

5. The path of freedom/no more learning (Vimuktimarga): This stage the Bodhisattva has completely purified themselves.

The Ten Bhumis (Stages of a Bodhisattva):

1. The joyous (Pramudita): Pramudita is attained in the Darshanamarga stage (path of seeing). It is attained by the direct perception of emptiness into reality. The bodhisattva works at the perfection of generosity (the first of the Six Perfections) and develops the ability to give away everything without regret and with no thought of praise or reward for themselves. All phenomena are viewed as empty and are subject to decay, suffering, and death, and so bodhisattvas lose all attachment to them. First level bodhisattvas directly understand that persons do not exist in and of themselves (by way of their own nature). Due to this, they overcome the false idea that the five aggregates constitute a truly existent person. The bodhisattvas train in ethics in order to cleanse their minds of negativity.

2. The stainless (Vimala): The bodhisattvas perfect ethics and overcome all tendencies towards engagement in negative actions. Their control becomes so complete that even in dreams they have no immoral thoughts. According to Nagarjuna:

The second is called the Stainless because all ten [virtuous] actions of body, speech and mind are stainless, And they naturally abide in those [deeds of ethics]. Through the maturation of those [good qualities], The perfection of ethics becomes supreme. They become Universal Monarchs helping beings, Masters of the glorious four continents and of the seven precious objects.

3. The light maker/the luminous (Prabhakari): Bodhisattvas on this level cultivate the perfection of patience. Trainees on the third level overcome all tendencies toward anger, and never react with hatred (or even annoyance) to any harmful acts or words. Rather, their equanimity remains constant, and all sentient beings are viewed with love and compassion. All anger and resentment rebound on the person who generates them, and they do nothing to eliminate harms that one has already experienced. They are counterproductive in that they destroy one's peace of mind and lead to unfavorable future situations. There is nothing to be gained by anger and resentment; revenge does nothing to change the past, and so the bodhisattva avoids them. Moreover, one's present suffering is only a result of one's own past misdeeds; so one's enemy is only an agent of the inevitable fruition of karma.

4. The radiant (Arcismati): On this level, the bodhisattvas cultivate the perfection of effort and eliminate afflictions. Bodhisattvas on this level burn up the afflictive obstructions and the obstructions to omniscience with the radiance of their wisdom. They enter into progressively deeper meditative absorptions and attain a powerful mental pliancy as a result. This eliminates laziness and increases their ability to practice meditation for extended periods of time.

5. The very hard to conquer/Difficult to cultivate (Sudurjaya): The fifth level is "difficult" because it involves practices that are so difficult and require a great deal of effort to perfect. It is also called the "Difficult to Overcome" because when one has completed the training of this level, one has profound wisdom and insight that are difficult to surpass or undermine. According to Nagarjuna:

The fifth is called the Extremely Difficult to Overcome
Since all evil ones find it extremely hard to conquer him;
He becomes skilled in knowing the subtle
Meanings of the noble truths and so forth.

Bodhisattvas on this level cultivate the perfection of Samadhi. They develop strong powers of meditative stabilization and overcome tendencies toward distraction. They achieve mental one-pointedness, and they perfect calm abiding. They also fully penetrate the meanings of the four noble truths and the two truths (conventional truths and ultimate truths) and perceive all phenomena as empty, transient and prone to suffering.

6. The turning towards/The manifest (Abhimukhi): On this level, the bodhisattva clearly perceives the workings of dependent arising and directly understands "signlessness." Signlessness refers to the fact that phenomena seem to possess their apparent qualities by way of their own nature, but when one examines this appearance, one realizes that all qualities are merely mentally imputed and not a part of the nature of the objects they appear to characterize. As a result of these understandings, bodhisattvas manifest meditative wisdom and avoid attachment to either cyclic existence or nirvana. Having overcome all attachments, bodhisattvas on this level can attain nirvana, but because of the force of the mind of awakening, they decide to remain in the world in order to benefit other sentient beings. They cultivate the Perfection of Wisdom, through which they perceive all phenomena as lacking inherent existence, as being like dreams, illusions, reflections, or magically created objects. All notions of "I" and "other" are transcended, along with conceptions of "inherent existence" and "inherent nonexistence." These sixth-level bodhisattvas abide in contemplation of suchness, with minds that are undisturbed by false ideas.

7. The far going/Gone afar (Durangama):
Bodhisattvas on the seventh level develop the ability to contemplate singleness uninterruptedly and enter into advanced meditative absorptions for extended periods of time, thus passing beyond both the mundane and supramundane paths of Sravakas and Pratyekabuddhas

(hearers and solitary realizers). For this reason, this level is called the "Gone Afar." According to Nagarjuna:

The seventh is the Gone Afar because
The number of his qualities has increased,
Moment by moment he can enter
The equipoise of cessation.

On this level, bodhisattvas perfect their skill in means of meditation and practice, which is their ability to cleverly adapt their teaching tactics to the individual proclivities and needs of their audiences. They also develop the ability to know the thoughts of others and in every moment are able to practice all the perfections. All thoughts and actions are free from afflictions, and they constantly act spontaneously and effectively for the benefit of others.

8. The unshakeable/The Immovable (Acala): The eighth level is called the "Immovable" because bodhisattvas overcome all afflictions regarding signs and their minds are always completely absorbed in the dharma. At this stage, the bodhisattva has attained realization equivalent to a Theravada Arhat. At this level, a bodhisattva has achieved nirvana. According to Nargarjuna:

The eighth is the Immovable, the youthful stage,
Through nonconceptuality he is immovable;
And the spheres of his body, speech and mind's
Activities are inconceivable.

Because they are fully acquainted with signlessness, their minds are not moved by ideas of signs. Eighth Bhumi bodhisattvas are said to be "irreversible," because there is no longer any possibility that they might waver on the path or backslide. They are destined for full Buddhahood, and there are no longer any inclinations to seek a personal nirvana. They cultivate the "perfection of aspiration," which means that they undertake to fulfill various vows, due to which they accumulate the causes of further virtues. Although they resolve to work for the benefit of others, and they pervade the universe with feelings of friendliness toward all sentient beings, these bodhisattvas have transcended any tendency to misunderstand anatta.

Their understanding of emptiness is so complete that it overturns innate delusions, and reality appears in a completely new light. They enter into meditation on emptiness with little effort. Bodhisattvas on this level are compared to people who have awakened from dreams, and all their perceptions are influenced by this new awareness. They attain the meditative state called "forbearance regarding non-arisen phenomena," due to which they no longer think in terms of inherent causes or inherent causelessness. They also develop the ability to manifest in various forms in order to instruct others. Compassion and skillful means are automatic and spontaneous. There is no need to plan or contemplate how best to benefit others since bodhisattvas on the eighth level automatically react correctly to every situation.

9. The good mind/The good intelligence (Sadhumati): From this point on, bodhisattvas move quickly toward awakening. Before this stage, progress was comparatively slow, like that of a boat being towed through a harbor. On the eighth through the tenth stage, however, bodhisattvas make huge strides toward Buddhahood, like a ship that reaches the ocean and unfurls its sails. On the ninth level, they fully understand the three vehicles: hearers, solitary realizers, and bodhisattvas - and perfect the ability to teach the doctrine. According to the *Sutra Explaining the Thought:*

Because of attaining faultlessness and very extensive intelligence in terms of mastery of teaching the doctrine in all aspects, the ninth level is called the "Good Intelligence."

Ninth level bodhisattvas also acquire the "four analytical knowledges": of fundamental concepts, meaning, grammar, and exposition. Due to this, they develop wondrous eloquence and skill in presenting doctrinal teachings. Their intelligence surpasses that of all humans and gods, and they comprehend all names, words, meanings, and languages. They can understand any question from any being. They also have the ability to answer them with a single sound, which is understood by each being according to its capacities. On this level, they also cultivate the perfection of virya (energy), which means that because of the strength of their mastery of the four analytical knowledges and their meditation they are able to develop paramitas energetically and to practice them continually without becoming fatigued.

10. The cloud of Dharma (Dharmamegha): This level is the level immediately before Buddhahood in which the last traces of afflictions are taken away. Like a cloud that pours rain on the earth, these bodhisattvas spread the dharma in all directions and each sentient being absorbs what it needs in order to grow spiritually. Thus, Nargarjuna states that:

> *The tenth is the Cloud of Dharma because*
> *The rain of excellent doctrine falls,*

The Bodhisattva is consecrated
With light by the Buddhas.

At this stage, bodhisattvas enter into progressively deeper meditative absorptions and develop limitless powers with respect to magical formulas. They cultivate the perfection of exalted wisdom, which enables them to increase their exalted wisdom. This, in turn, strengthens the other perfections. As a result, they become established in the joy of the doctrine.

They acquire perfect bodies, and their minds are cleansed of the subtlest traces of the afflictions. They manifest in limitless forms for the benefit of others and transcend the ordinary laws of time and space. They are able to place entire world systems in a single pore without diminishing them or increasing the size of the pore. When they do this, the beings inhabiting the worlds feel no discomfort and only those who are advanced bodhisattvas even notice.

Bodhisattvas on this level receive a form of empowerment from innumerable buddhas. This is called "great rays of light," because the radiance of these bodhisattvas shines in all directions. This empowerment helps them in removing the remaining obstructions to omniscience and gives them added confidence and strength. At the final moment of this stage, they enter into a meditative state called the "vajralike meditative stabilization," in which the subtlest remaining obstacles to Buddhahood are overcome. When they arise from this concentration, they arise as Buddhas!

What are the three poisons?

In Buddhism, the Three Poisons – or the three unwholesome roots or the three fires – refer to ignorance, greed, and anger. Ignorance, greed, and anger are deeply embedded in the conditioning of our personalities. Our behavior is habitually influenced and tainted by these three poisons; these unwholesome roots buried deep into our mind. Burning within us as lust, craving, anger, resentment and misunderstanding, these poisons lay to waste hearts, lives, hopes, and civilizations, driving us blind and thirsty through the seemingly endless round of birth and death (samsara). The Buddha describes these defilements as bonds, fetters, hindrances, and knots; the actual root cause of unwholesome karma and the entire spectrum of human suffering.

Although this teaching may appear negative or unpleasant, a wise understanding of the three poisons of ignorance, greed and anger is ultimately positive and empowering. With this sublime understanding, we can clearly see and feel the factors that are causing confusion, unhappiness, and suffering in our lives. And with this

196

clarity and insight, we can make the choice to eliminate those factors! The teaching of The Four Noble Truths clearly explains that when we embrace and understand the exact causes of our suffering and dissatisfaction, we can then take the necessary steps to extinguish those causes and liberate ourselves. This is certainly positive and empowering.

In addition to meditation practice, there are also the antidotes or alternatives to the three poisons. For every defilement, the Buddha has given us the antidote, the method whereby we eliminate unwholesome mental attitudes and replace them with virtuous, wholesome attitudes which benefit ourselves and others. Therefore, the entire aim of spiritual practice is to gradually subdue the poisons of ignorance, greed and anger by cultivating the alternative mental factors that are directly opposed to them. These antidotes are called the three wholesome roots: non-ignorance, non-greed, and non-anger.

Ignorance

Ignorance, or delusion, is our wrong understanding or wrong views of reality. Ignorance is our misperception of the way the world works; our inability to understand the nature of things exactly as they are, free of perceptual distortions. Influenced by ignorance, we are not in harmony with ourselves, others, or with life; we are not living in accordance with Dharma. Affected by the poison of delusion, which arises from ignorance of our true nature, we do not understand the interdependent and impermanent nature of life. Thus, we are constantly looking outside of ourselves for happiness, satisfaction and solutions to our problems. This outward searching creates even more frustration, anger and delusion. Because of our ignorance, we also do not understand the virtuous, life-affirming actions that create happiness, nor do we understand the non-virtuous, negative and unwholesome actions that create suffering. Again, our ignorance binds us to a vicious cycle where there does not appear to be any way out.

To antidote and overcome ignorance and delusion, we cultivate wisdom, insight, and right understanding. Learning to experience reality exactly as it is, without the distortions of our self-centered desires, fears and expectations, we free ourselves from delusion. Deeply sensing and acting in harmony with the interdependent, impermanent and ever-changing nature of this world— realizing that all living beings are inseparably related and that lasting happiness does not come from anything external—we free ourselves from delusion. As we develop a clear understanding of karma, knowing the positive, wholesome actions that bring happiness and the negative, unwholesome actions that bring suffering, we cultivate the wisdom, insight and right understanding that free us from ignorance and delusion.

Greed

Our greed is a burning desire, an unquenchable thirst (tanha), craving and lust; we want the objects of our desire to provide us with lasting satisfaction, so we feel fulfilled, whole and complete. The poison of greed creates an inner hunger so that we always seem to be striving towards an unattainable goal. We mistakenly believe our happiness is dependent upon that goal, but once we attain it, we get no lasting satisfaction. Then once again, our greed and desire will arise, looking outside of ourselves for the next thing that will hopefully bring satisfaction. Influenced by greed, we are never content. Another common face of our greed shows up as a lack of generosity and compassion toward others. Even a moment of honest and mindful introspection will reveal how deeply-rooted our greed can be. We can experience the symptoms of our greed appearing in even the most trivial instances, and of course, greed can manifest itself in even more compulsive and destructive ways as well. We always seem to want more, we want bigger and better things, we want to fulfill our insatiable inner hunger and thirst (craving). This type of greed affects our personal lives, our professional lives and the domain of international business and politics. Global conflict and

warfare, as well as the destruction of our precious
environment, are obvious symptoms of our corporate
and political greed. Our greed, craving and thirst affect
each of us on a personal and global level. Our greed is an
endless and damaging cycle that only brings suffering
and unhappiness in its wake.

<u>To antidote and overcome greed</u>, we learn to
cultivate selflessness, generosity, non-attachment and
contentment. If we are experiencing greed, strong desire,
or attachment and we want to let it go, we can
contemplate the impermanence or the disadvantages of
the objects of our desire. We can practice giving away
those things we would most like to hold onto. We can
also practice acts of selfless service and charity, offering
care and assistance to others in any way we can, free of
all desire for recognition or compensation. In truth, there
is no objection to enjoying and sharing the beauty,
pleasures, and objects of this material world. The
problems associated with greed and attachment only arise
when we mistakenly believe and act as if the source of
our happiness is outside of ourselves.

Anger

The symptoms of anger can show up as hatred,
hostility, dislike, aversion, or ill will; wishing harm or
suffering upon another person. With aversion, we

habitually resist, deny and avoid unpleasant feelings, circumstances and people we do not like. We want everything to be pleasant, comfortable and satisfying all the time. This behavior simply reinforces our perception of duality and separation. Hatred or anger thrusts us into a vicious cycle of always finding conflict and enemies everywhere around us. When there is conflict or perceived enemies around us, our mind is neurotic, never calm and we are endlessly occupied with strategies of self-protection or revenge. We can also create conflict within ourselves when we have an aversion to our own uncomfortable feelings. With hatred and aversion, we deny, resist and push away our own inner feelings of fear, hurt, loneliness and so forth, treating these feelings like an internal enemy. With the poison of anger, we create conflict and enemies in the world around us and within our own being.

To antidote and overcome anger and hatred, we learn to cultivate loving-kindness, compassion, patience and forgiveness. When we react to unpleasant feelings, circumstances, or people, with hatred, anger, or aversion, we can use these sublime antidotes to counteract the poisons. Here we learn to openly embrace the entire spectrum of our experiences without hatred or aversion. Just as we practice meeting unpleasant experiences in the outer world with patience, kindness, forgiveness, and compassion, we must also practice meeting our own unpleasant feelings in the same way. Our feelings of loneliness, hurt, doubt, fear, insecurity, inadequacy, depression and so forth, all require our openness and loving-kindness. Our challenge in spiritual practice is to soften our habitual defenses, open our heart, and let go of hatred, aversion and denial. In this way, we can meet and embrace ourselves, others and all inner and outer experiences with great compassion and wisdom.

I see a lot of people are or become "Buddhists" and phase out of it, or think they've found their answer then move on from Buddhism. Others have suddenly become Buddhists. Is it that easy to be a Buddhist?

If we really had to point it out, we can say that there are six "kinds" of Buddhists. Some of these Buddhists are born Buddhists; other find it while some just think it's cool. Titling ourselves as Buddhist is like titling ourselves as one of the "cool kids" at school; it's a big deal, and we're excited we're part of something everyone knows.

But to a true Buddhist practitioner, the title should be the least of your concerns. If someone asked me what my religion was, I will say "spiritual." Only if they asked for a specific practice will I say Buddhism, but to me, this title or path is not concerning to anyone else but myself. In Buddhism, we try to eradicate titles, because for every title we add and accumulate, the more attachment we have to suffer with. A lot of new people to Buddhism get very attached to "being Buddhist" because of its popularity and superficial assumption that practicing Buddhism automatically makes us happy and peaceful.

The six "kinds" of Buddhists are:

1.   People who are born into Buddhism. A huge population of Asian countries are Buddhists, so a person born into a Buddhist family will grow up learning and practicing Buddhism.

2.   People who marry a person who is Buddhist. Not always the case that if we marry someone who is Buddhist we too will become Buddhist, but a lot of soldiers in the Vietnam war, for example, who married Vietnamese women that were Buddhist often also converted to Buddhism to create a connection and bond with someone who they could barely understand.

3.   People that find Buddhism. For many, Buddhism was stumbled upon. Perhaps through a World Religions class in college, passing by a Buddhist temple, watching a Buddhist documentary, or interacting with

someone who is Buddhist.

4.   People that claim to be "Buddhist" because it's the newest, coolest thing to be. The recent popularity of Buddhism within the last 50 years has greatly increased in the West. With the help of the H.H. the Dalai Lama, Tibetan Buddhism is one of the most "popular" forms of Buddhism in the West, as well Zen Buddhism. Because of the popularity of the Dalai Lama, this created popularity for Buddhism, which in turn created this assumption that if one became Buddhist, they too would be part of this "popular" group.

5.   People who go to Buddhism for happiness and peace. A major misconception of Buddhism is that if we become Buddhists, then we would magically defeat depression, sadness, anger, and suffering. What people don't understand, what most people don't understand, is that Buddhism is not a magic happiness pill. It is not a path where we can cleanse the sadness away by simply claiming to be Buddhist. What Buddhism actually is, is a set of instructions and guides to help us be on a path of happiness and peace.

6.   People who claim to be Buddhist, but don't practice. If we study without practice, we become scholars. If we practice without studying, we become

superstitious. In many Buddhist temples, the head monk or teacher will tell their new students that they need to study and attend the temple for a minimum of one year before they can take their refuge and precept vows. And a minimum of another two years before they can take their Bodhisattva vows. Why? Because Buddhism is a lot of work! Buddhist practice and study are intense, profound, complex and eye-opening if practiced correctly. But we often see people calling themselves "Buddhist" but then do not practice any of the precepts or the eightfold path.

If we practice Buddhism and call ourselves Buddhists, then we need to be practicing for the right reasons. Everyone wants to be happy and at peace, but "being into Buddhism" won't make us happy and peaceful. It takes work, effort and diligence to overcome the slightest dissatisfactions of the world. Buddhism can help, but only with diligent and sincere practice.

Part VIII

Buddha, Bodhisattvas and Enlightenment

What Is Buddha Nature?

Buddha Nature is the potential that all sentient beings can attain full enlightenment, to become Buddhas. Every living being has Buddha-Nature and has the ability to perfect and eradicate all defilements of their mind. Everyone has Buddha Nature. It is like fresh air that's available to everyone – it doesn't discriminate or pick and choose between who does and doesn't get air, every living being has access to it.

Likewise, Buddha Nature does not discriminate, and we all have it. We reach its full potential with practice and cleansing our mind of negative thoughts, emotions and attitudes.

So those who practice Buddhism, worship Buddha, a statue of a man who once lived, correct? I was

207

never sure. And also, do you all believe that Buddha is the one true God? Or do you believe in God at all?

Buddha was not and is not a god. He was a human being just like the rest of us who realized the path to escape suffering. Buddhists do not worship Buddha. We bow to his statue, image or name out of respect and humility, and a way of thanks for the teachings he gave and passed down to us.

Buddhists believe in different things. Generally, the concept of a God or deity is not important in Buddhism, because we don't rely on external forces or circumstances for our liberation or future. Only we can control how and what our lives become, by our own determination, efforts, and actions.

What is a Bodhisattva and Bodhicitta?

A Bodhisattva is the ideal practitioner in Mahayana Buddhism and Bodhicitta is the altruistic wish to realize enlightenment for the benefit of all beings. A Bodhisattva is an enlightened being or a being on the path of enlightenment. An enlightened bodhisattva has already escaped the prison of Samsara, the cycle of life and death, but out of their great compassion for all beings,

208

they choose to be reborn again for the sake of helping others also realize enlightenment.

We can all become bodhisattvas, and we can all develop bodhicitta. The development of bodhicitta is a gradual one. Sometimes it comes in very short moments, a few seconds maybe. As we practice more and develop our bodhicitta, it lasts longer and longer until our bodhicitta is fully developed.

Isn't "aspiring" to be a bodhisattva contradictory? Wouldn't that mean you are desiring/craving enlightenment?

Not all desire is bad. Good desire can also mean "motivation," because we must have the desire and motivation to want to become a Buddha! After all, that is the goal of Buddhism!

As long as we don't attach to the Dharma and to our practices, we can always aspire to reach Buddhahood. Because once we become a Buddha, the dharma is no longer necessary! The dharma is simply the guide to reach Buddhahood, and once it's reached, we won't need the guide anymore. Buddhism is like the tools we need to build a house; the wood, nails, hammers, cement, paint, etc. We build and build until the house is complete and we can give away our extra tools to those who need it.

Likewise, we build and develop our knowledge and aspiration for Buddhahood until it's reached, and once we get there, we use our knowledge to aspire and help others.

We are all aspiring Bodhisattvas who aspire to become Buddhas! That is our goal. So we must have some desire in order to reach and accomplish that goal.

What does faith mean in Buddhism?

I'm sure growing up as Christians, Catholics, or Muslims, the word "faith" pops up a lot. "Have faith in God," "Have faith in Jesus," etc. Those religions rely on these outside sources to somehow fuel our "faith-o-meter" in something or someone, whether we're waiting on results for a test, a decision on a home mortgage loan, or maybe because things in our life just aren't happening. People always seem to put their faith in someone else's hands.

In Buddhism we have faith. But it's not in the Buddha or any of the Bodhisattvas. Buddha is not a god or deity of worship. Buddha never asked us to worship him or give him offerings, and he never asked us to ask him for blessings. He doesn't accept bribery. Buddha said, "If you want to serve me, do so by serving the people."

210

So what faith does Buddhism have? Faith in Buddhism is faith in ourselves. It's faith in ourselves in knowing we have the potential, the aspiration, the Buddha Nature, to become a Buddha someday! We, and all sentient beings have Buddha Nature. Buddha Nature is the innate capacity we all have to achieve Buddhahood.

It's important to not only follow and live a life as a Buddhist practitioner but to also believe that we will someday become a Buddha. That might happen in this life, the next life, or the next several lives – but it will eventually happen. As long as we practice the Eightfold Path, we guarantee ourselves a closer chance to achieving liberation.

So unlike in other religions where they rely on a god, prophet, or some sort of deity of worship, Buddhism is a mind-centered religion. It's an "I can help myself" religion – we don't need permission, blessings, or forgiveness from anyone else, all we need to do is ask ourselves, "Is this right thought/perception/action, etc.?" And if we've done something "wrong," we don't need to seek forgiveness from the Buddha or a monk, we simply forgive ourselves and promise ourselves we'll not do it again (or, at least, try not to!).

What did The Buddha realize the night he attained enlightenment under the Bodhi tree? Was it paticcasamuppada or the four noble truths? What is Idapaccayata?

The Buddha wanted to know how to get out of the cycle of suffering; he wanted to know how to end it. He had a lavish lifestyle growing up as a prince and still saw suffering, and then tried extreme asceticism and still could not find the answer to his question. Then he realized the Middle Way. When he gained Enlightenment, he gained the knowledge of the Four Noble Truths; the means of ending suffering, and from it the Eightfold Path; the path to ending suffering.

Buddha preached about Pratityasamutpada (dependent origination) later on when he turned the Dharma Wheel.

Idapaccayata can roughly be translated as the conditioned nature of things or the universal principle of conditionality. Basically the cause and effect of things. It refers to the principle of causality–that all things arise and exist due to certain causes (or conditions) and cease once these causes (or conditions) are removed.

"This is because that is.
This is not, because that is not.
This ceases to be because that ceases to be.

212

In the Lotus Sutra, Buddha speaks of three vehicles that were inferior; the Lotus being the culmination of these teachings. Please explain.

The Buddha taught the Dharma to the people according to their understanding/intelligence capacity. Buddha first preached the various provisional teachings, or the three vehicle teachings, as an expedient means to help people develop the capacity to understand and receive the one vehicle teaching; the vehicle of Buddhahood. In the Lotus Sutra, he declares that the earlier teachings have been set forth as expedient means to prepare people for the teaching of the sutra, which is the supreme vehicle of Buddhahood, the goal of the Buddhist practice. This concept is expressed as the replacement of the three vehicles with the one vehicle.

The Three Vehicles mentioned in the Lotus Sutra represents the Sravakas, Pratykabuddhas, and Bodhisattvas.

Sravaka means "hearer" or "disciple." Sravakas are of the "four assemblies": monks, nuns, laymen, and laywomen. So we, as lay followers, would be considered a Sravaka.

Pratykabuddha is a Buddha "on their own." These are the people who attain Enlightenment on their own without a teacher teaching the Dharma. If we didn't have Sakyamuni Buddha as our teacher and we reached Enlightenment, we would be a Pratykabuddha. A

Pratykabuddha is one of three types of enlightened beings. The other two are Arahats, those who have found liberation out of the cycle of Samsara; and Samyaksambuddhas, which is similar to Pratykabuddhas as far as finding Enlightenment on their own, but Samyaksambuddhas preach the Dharma they discovered, whereas Pratykabuddhas don't. The Historical Sakyamuni Buddha is considered a Samyaksambuddha.

Bodhisattva is anyone who has great aspiration to cultivate compassion, Bodhicitta and attain Buddhahood for the benefit of all sentient beings. Becoming a Bodhisattva is the goal in Mahayana and Tibetan Buddhism; to be reborn an infinite amount of times to liberate all sentient beings from Samsara. A Bodhisattva works on the Six Perfections (Paramitas): Generosity, Patience, Virtue, Effort, Meditation, and Insight (Wisdom).

Can knowledge only liberate? I like reading books on spirituality, Buddhism, and other philosophical subjects. But still I feel I am missing something in life.

Knowledge can only do so much for us. If we're simply reading without practicing, then we're just a scholar; we know all the information, but we don't really know how it works. In Buddhism, the way we liberate ourselves is through practice. Regular meditation, practicing the eightfold path, and using the knowledge we read will lead us to the wisdom of enlightenment!

We already know the purpose of our life. That purpose is to get out of the cycle of birth and death! We want to stop being reborn in this cyclic existence and be free from it! To liberate ourselves from attachment, ignorance, and anger that keeps us in Samsara. In Buddhism, studying and practicing is a life-long journey. Just because we read dozens of books on different topics doesn't mean anything if we don't apply those topics to our everyday life. In Buddhism, we never stop learning. Buddhism is so profound, so complex with so much information; it's extremely difficult to cover all the topics in one or two years. It takes a lifetime!

So really, we're not missing anything in life. The purpose of our life is to gain the knowledge we need to be and stay on the path of liberation. When we have that knowledge, we must apply it. Whenever we read something, we need to meditate on it afterward and contemplate it. It is only during meditation that our contemplation can turn into wisdom, and it is only wisdom that can lead us to enlightenment!

Don't rush. In modern society, everyone's in a hurry, everyone's running and trying to stop time because they think their lives are so busy, but it's not true. Time does not go faster when we try to rush. So just be patient and continue studying, but we must apply it! Otherwise, the backpack we carry all our books in is going to be very heavy and slow us down!

If Buddha says we should not believe anything even if he has said it, we should find out for ourselves, and people say that drugs which alter your consciousness and does not agree with the precepts, does this mean one must experience drugs for themselves? This was contradicting to me and made me confused because if we shouldn't intake drugs which take away our control, yet we only know they are bad because others have said it, should we try it?

Drugs aren't bad because others have *said* it, it's bad because we can *see* the consequences and unfortunate events it can do to people – worst case scenario, death. The five precepts are not rules or regulations. The precepts are common sense; do not kill, steal, lie, commit sexual misconduct, and intake intoxicants. Why would we need to experience them to determine if they're good or bad? It's already obvious (or, at least, it should be) that they are things we should avoid.

The precepts aren't even the Buddha's creation. Since there were no "rules" in the sangha, after several monks got in trouble for having sex, getting drunk and taking life, the Buddha asked the sangha to come up with some "suggestions" for the monastics to live by, and so the precepts were created.

The Buddha was specifically talking about certain teachings when he said to not believe him and to explore it for ourselves. In most cases it was meditation methods and anything that required our own contemplation and observation.

What is the best way to find my path to enlightenment?

By not looking for it!

Enlightenment is already here. We just have to clear the dust on the glass that's blocking our view.

Understanding the Four Noble Truths and practicing the Eightfold Path is the rag that will help you clean the dirty glass for a clear view of reality and the Truth.

I want to reach Bodhi, but I don't want to isolate myself from modern life, as in friends not

necessarily tech.. I just want to reach perfect existence without shaving my head and exclusively wearing orange robes.

I don't know what you're reading, but the Buddha never said you have to abandon your normal life to practice Buddhism or any other path. Modern life and everything in it is a million times more distracting than the time of the Buddha when they had not even a fraction of what we have today, and it was still difficult for some people to reach enlightenment.

We probably won't realize enlightenment in this life or for the next few hundred or thousands because life after life we've accumulated more and more dust, that's covering the path to enlightenment. But with diligence and conviction, we can help sweep away some of the dust on the path so we can see what way it leads.

Don't focus on trying to reach "perfect existence." There's really no such thing, and it probably won't happen in this life. We have way too many distractions and defilements to eradicate before we can even reach the stepping stones of a liberated life. For now, focus on the actual practice. Read, study and practice. If you try too hard to reach the non-existent finish line, then you'll never get there.

Part IX

Becoming a Buddhist, Sex and Vegetarianism

Are Buddhists vegetarian?

Many Buddhists are vegetarian. Most monastics in Mahayana Buddhism are. However, some Buddhists in Japan and the monasteries of Theravada Buddhism are not vegetarian. The Buddha was not a vegetarian, nor did he say we had to be vegetarian. Because he lived in a geographical area where agriculture wasn't the best, he lived off whatever alms people gave him. He never said, "I'm a vegetarian, don't give me meat." The whole point of almsgiving is to accept whatever is offered to you.

Visiting a Mahayana Buddhist temple and staying for lunch or dinner, the meal will almost always be vegetarian. Mahayana advocates for vegetarianism, but they won't force you to do it. It is simply being compassionate towards all living beings. Even though you might sit down at a restaurant and order a steak and say to ourselves, "But it's already dead anyway." It might be dead already, but then we are contributing to the death

219

of the next animal. In this case, it's all about supply and demand. The more people go into restaurants and order steak, the more the restaurant will have to order more steak, and the more animals the supplier will have to kill.

If we are not vegetarian, we can, at least, be mindful and thankful of the meat we do eat. Mindful that we are eating meat and that it died for us, and thankful that the animal's life is able to provide us the necessary nutrients and energy to survive and practice the Dharma.

As of late, I have felt myself being more and more drawn to Buddhism. I don't know if it's a desire to a Buddhist myself but I was just in need of some sort of help, I guess. I have no religion, and my relationship with any god is odd. I just need some sort of guidance from someone.

Buddhism is a draw to a lot of people because of it's peaceful, compassionate and almost hippie-like nature. There are many debates on whether or not Buddhism is a religion, philosophy or way of life. In my opinion, it is a religion, philosophy and a way of life, but at the same time is not. It's kind of hard to really put a term on it because it's very scientific, but it's also very philosophical. So it attracts a lot of different people for different reasons.

You don't have to be Buddhist to practice Buddhism. If you're Christian and interested in Buddhism, Buddhism will make you a better Christian. If you're Catholic, Buddhism will help you become a better Catholic. In general, Buddhism will help you become a better person. There are many things in Buddhism that you can use to simply better yourself and life, like applying the Eightfold Path and practicing meditation. These steps are simple Buddhist approaches to having a better, calmer life.

As for being an actual Buddhist, there's a lot of work and study involved. There are so many important texts to read, learn and understand. Profound concepts like emptiness, the five aggregates, dependent origination, etc. that we must study throughout life. Because Buddhism doesn't have a concept of a God, you are your own god. So the point in life isn't just to find happiness and peace, but to also find yourself, find your inner god, your Buddha Nature. It's all about self-development and self-realization. Buddhists don't pray to a god or a deity to ask for help, guidance, or a better life – you ask yourself, give yourself the initial motivation and better your life yourself. No one is in charge of your life but yourself.

What are Buddhists' thoughts on homosexuality?

Buddhism says nothing about homosexuality and gay marriage. Buddha taught us to love and respect everyone, regardless of race, color, social class, sexual orientation, royal status, etc. The only "kind" of Buddhism where it is mentioned is in Tibetan Buddhism where homosexuality (for ordained monks/nuns) is forbidden, but sex is forbidden anyway, so it almost contradicts itself.

Homosexuality and gay marriage are acceptable or non-acceptable according to the society Buddhism is in. If we're in a country where gay marriage is legal and socially acceptable, then it is acceptable to Buddhism in that country. If we're in a country where gay marriage is illegal and is socially not acceptable, Buddhism will still accept it, but they might not accept us to ordain or conduct a marriage ceremony.

In some Buddhist traditions/countries asking if we are homosexual is one of the questions asked during the ordination process. It may or may not affect their decision to accept us. However it is usually not a big deal since Buddhism clearly teaches us to love every sentient being, especially those who we see as enemies or in this case, "different."

I think it was in 2013 that Taiwan had its first Buddhist gay wedding. From what I can remember, I think it was the first anywhere. So it is possible, depending on where we live. In the states, however, because Buddhist temples are mostly oriental (Chinese, Vietnamese, Tibetan, or Thai) where gay marriage is usually unacceptable in their home countries, they might not allow it here either. It really all depends on where we are and who we ask.

Bottom line: Buddhism has no mention at all of homosexuality. The Buddhist Vinaya (the "rules" of monastic living) forbids sex or any sexual acts, so it doesn't matter what orientation you are.

I've done lots of research and read books on Buddhism. I am truly interested, but it's hard incorporating everything into my everyday life. What do you recommend?

Take it step-by-step. Don't rush. If we rush, we'll never learn and really absorb anything. There's so much to learn and practice in Buddhism; it takes a whole lifetime to really grasp just a handful of ideas and concepts.

First, it's important that we really have a strong understanding of the foundations of Buddhism: the four noble truths, eightfold path, karma, meditation and the twelve links of dependent origination. These are the pillars that hold up everything else in Buddhism. So it's important to spend several years just on these few concepts before moving on to more challenging and comprehensive topics.

We should spend anywhere from one week to one month, or longer, on each of the topics, because it really does take that long to fully understand each noble truth and each section of every other topic. Meditate on each topic, contemplate its meaning – how it was described to us and what it means to us. Meditating on the first noble truth for a month might seem ridiculous, but something that seems so "simple" as "Life is suffering" is actually a very profound teaching.

Ask ourselves, "What is life? What is suffering?" Deep meditation on these questions can open up our minds to great wisdom and pave the path towards enlightenment. As Buddhists, we're constantly learning and developing. We never stop studying or learning new things. We could live up to 100 years and have only read a quarter of Buddhist scriptures!

Never stop reading. Never stop learning. The more we learn, the more wisdom we have, and the easier we can reach enlightenment.

I have a strong urge to change my spiritual beliefs. I grew up in Catholic Church and then converted

into Lutheran. I can't seem to follow through with these religions. However, I do believe in a God. I struggle with believing in something that makes sense, and so far I find myself leaning toward Buddhism. How can I begin to do this? What should I do to remain in the right path to do so?

As with any path, religion or spirituality, it's very personal. Modern religion (for the most part) has strayed away from strict, 'we're going to follow the same rules that were put down thousands of years ago,' ordeal and make up our own rules. For Christians, Catholics, Muslims, etc. they break their own rules on a daily basis because ancient rules don't apply in today's age.

With Buddhism on the other hand, it's the kind of religion that needs to change according to the societal and local customs. That's why Buddhism is different in almost every country. It's still all Buddhism; believing, practicing and reading the same Dharma, but Buddhism in India is very different than Buddhism in China. With that said, you can still be a Christian and practice a Buddhist way. Being a Christian and practicing Buddhist philosophy of non-violence, loving-compassion and loving-kindness simply makes you a better Christian.

To be a Buddhist, a true, devout Buddhist is an effort to learning and practicing its profound philosophy, sutras, and Dharma. But by taking certain concepts of Buddhism like non-violence, love, compassion and loving-kindness, and applying it to your own life and religion, that just makes you a better person and a better follower of your own religion. Buddhism gives you the simple path of living a better, happier life.

Buddhism doesn't have a concept of a God or a need for it. It's a mind-centered religion where we are our own judge and responsible for our own suffering and happiness. So without having to "convert" to Buddhism, use Buddhist practices of loving-kindness and compassion. Grab an intro book of Buddhism like *The Heart of the Buddha's Teaching* by Thich Nhat Hanh, for a little more in-depth knowledge. Practice what we read and know, and apply it to our own beliefs.

Our life isn't about bettering it or making it satisfactory for a god or some deity – it's about bettering it and satisfying it for our own benefit and then for the benefits of others; finding the causes of suffering, eliminating them, and being happy. We can't help others without helping ourselves first!

Being in a family life and taking care of family, can someone still aspire to become a bodhisattva? Family life is full of affliction of desire, attachment, wants, etc.

Of course! We can aspire to become a Buddha and

be the father of a household of twenty people! But the keyword here is *aspiring*! Many texts say it's important and even required to renounce and emancipate our current life in order to find true liberation. But because we probably won't find liberation or get to the level of Bodhisattva in this life, we can, at least, set the foundations and create the path toward it for our future lives.

We might not have many desires or attachments, but that doesn't mean a monastic would find liberation before us. Our Buddha Nature is just as equal as any monastic. We might be surrounded by all these distractions, whereas a monastic is not, but that doesn't mean they're better than us or vice-versa. We could be a better practitioner, maybe we have more virtuous merits – so as long as we aspire and *know* that we will find liberation, we will become a Buddha one day, that's all that matters.

All we can do is practice. If there's a local or nearby temple we can go to, visit often and attend their services. Temple is the one place where we can go and forget about all our worldly problems and just be at peace for a couple of hours. By regularly practicing meditation, we can learn to handle and ease the emotions that might arise by all the afflictions, desires and attachments that surround us.

I've read that the Dalai Lama is not okay with homosexuality. Is it true? And why so?

He's probably indifferent about the topic. He quotes, "from society's viewpoint, mutually agreeable homosexual relations can be of mutual benefit, enjoyable, and harmless." But he considers homosexuality in Buddhism to be "sexual misconduct." However, the rule also applies to heterosexuals because the rule forbids oral and anal sex, and masturbation. Though the "no homosexual" rule is only in Vajrayana (Tibetan Buddhism).

The Buddha never commented or made any remarks toward homosexuals. He viewed everyone to be equal, and everyone was equally qualified to gain enlightenment, gay or straight. Monastics are vowed to be celibate, so whether they're gay or straight doesn't really matter because they won't be having any sex anyway! For lay people following the five precepts, sexual misconduct doesn't mean no sex, it means no sex with someone we shouldn't be having sex with. We can ask ourselves, "Would I like this if someone did this to me?" "Does the act cause harm and regret instead of benefit and joy?" "Will the act harm or benefit the attainment of liberation?" "Is the act motivated by love, generosity, and understanding?"

Basically, the issue of homosexuality is only in some Tibetan traditions. Otherwise, it's not an important issue or a relevant one.

I was just wondering where Buddhists stand on issues like abortion and gay marriage? As well as sex before marriage?

Abortion is considered breaking the first Precept, no killing. So obviously, that's a no-no. Even in extreme situations such as rape, as horrible as that is, aborting the child will guarantee us an unfortunate rebirth (to hell according to some scriptures regarding taking life). In this case, the best option is to have the baby and give it up for adoption.

Buddhism does not discriminate against gender, religion, race, social class, caste, etc. So it does not discriminate against the rights of gays and gay marriage. Only in Tibetan Buddhism where homosexuality is forbidden for the monastics, but accepting for lay people. Otherwise, the Buddha never once mentioned homosexuality, so almost all Buddhist schools agree that it is neither right nor wrong. Because Buddhists regard everyone as equal, like our mothers, brothers, wives, sisters, fathers – why should we discriminate or hate anyone?

Sexual misconduct, one of the five precepts, is often the most confusing for people because it gives off a portrayal as no sex at all or something dramatic. What sexual misconduct actually refers to is to not be unfaithful, have sex with multiple partners or inappropriate sex (rape and sex with prostitutes). If we are in a relationship, we stay faithful to that person; having sex with only that person. The same regard goes for sex before marriage.

I really want to be a Buddhist, but I'm too afraid to tell my parents. I'm afraid they'll be mad or sad, but in my mind, I'm already a Buddhist. Can I go to vihara/temple if I'm not a Buddhist? I really want to talk to the monks, can I?

If in your mind you're already Buddhist, then why do you feel you have to tell anyone? If you feel the need to tell everyone, then you're not really a Buddhist. Calling ourselves a Buddhist is another title to add to our ego and then our ego will want to flaunt it and announce it to the world, pulling you deeper and deeper towards the wrong path.

A Buddhist that is not a Buddhist is a true Buddhist.

Anyone and everyone is welcome at Buddhist temples. Most temple visitors are not Buddhists and are simply curious people that want to experience and see something new and interesting. Many temples will usually serve lunch or dinner after services, and that is usually the opportunity to sit down with the Sangha and ask questions.

I want to convert my life and be a Buddhist but how?

You don't.

"Converting" to Buddhism doesn't make you a Buddhist, just like going to church doesn't make you a Christian. It's the practice and the way you live your life and treat others that make you a Buddhist.

When Christians, Jews or Catholics come to Buddhist practice, they don't practice to become Buddhists; they practice to become better practitioners of their own religion. Nothing about Buddhism is religious. Buddhism is mind-centered, not God-centered, so you can be anything and use Buddhist practices to make you a better person and live a better life.

I want to convert to Buddhism. I want to learn slowly but learn all I can. My pain and suffering doesn't allow me to move to a happier life. I have tried meditating, but I can't seem to get it right.

Sometimes I just feel so angry, and it's because of all the grudges I hold within me. I have thought of getting a tattoo of a Buddha to show that I have now found peace within the Buddha. But I'm not sure if that's a sign of disrespect towards the Buddha. Please help.

How can you say you've found peace with the Buddha if you're still angry and carrying grudges? Where's the peace?

I'm sure you and many, many, many others have this assumption that Buddhism is peace. That converting to Buddhism will somehow magically make their life happier and peaceful. Well, guess what? It doesn't. It actually makes your life much more complicated and harder because Buddhism forces you to confront yourself and your inner issues and problems, which for a while will cause a lot of sadness and anger and suffering.

Buddhism is not peace and happiness. Buddhism is the path that leads to peace and happiness. Buddhism is like a ladder. You need a ladder to reach the ceiling to change the light bulb. Otherwise, you can't reach, and you'll have to live in darkness. So you get a ladder and climb the steps to reach the ceiling. Sometimes you might slip and scrape your leg or knee, and you bleed. You get angry because this tool that's supposed to help you accomplish something is hurting you, but then you realize you need to be more careful and mindful of where

232

and how you're stepping. Eventually, you will reach the ceiling and change the light bulb.

Buddhism is like that. You have to actively find the tools necessary to achieve your goal. There might be bumps and bruises along the way, but with practice, commitment and diligence, your light bulb will go off, and then, nirvana.

So when you practice and meditate, you need to confront yourself and ask yourself why are you angry? Why are you holding grudges? What good is that doing for you? What happiness could this suffering possibly give you? Absolutely nothing. Don't try to fool yourself with superficial excuses like, "they hurt my feelings," "they went behind my back," "they lied to me," etc. Boohoo. That's life, crap happens, and you take what's being thrown at you, and it's your job to either dodge them and let it go, or catch them and hang on to its anger.

Life is as peaceful and blissful as you choose to make it. If all you see is anger, your life will always be in suffering. If you choose to see happiness, your life will always be in happiness.

So I'm discovering Buddhism and loving it and as I'm researching and reading it seems that many

***Buddhists are vegetarian… Would becoming a
vegetarian help me become more empathetic and
mindful towards all living things? Would it be
beneficial to my spiritual journey?***

You're going to get varying answers depending on
who you ask. So from my point of view and
understanding: No, vegetarianism is not necessary.

Sure, not eating meat could mean you're empathetic
towards animals and their lives, but unless you're helping
preserve the lives of animals, all you're doing is bringing
down the demand for meat (which is great regardless!).
We always see those sad videos and commercials about
animal cruelty, and we feel extremely sad about it. What
do we do? We change the channel or stop watching;
we're not actually helping or doing anything about it. So
how is your empathy helping?

Vegetarianism should mean something, and you
should actually do something about it, and not just for the
sake of being a vegetarian because you feel sad for
animals.

Nowhere in Buddhism (well, except maybe in a
couple of Chinese Mahayana sutras) does it mention that
we need to be vegetarian. Not even the Buddha was
vegetarian. The Buddha and his disciples went on alms
every day and ate what was given to them. They were
begging for food, so they had no right to be picky and
only ask for vegetarian food.

I'm not even vegetarian. I call myself a "Buddhist vegetarian." I'm vegetarian on my own and when I cook for myself, but if someone invites me over or out for lunch or dinner and offers me meat, then I must accept and eat it. I always say a prayer before meals, thanking those who have worked hard to make the food I'm about to eat possible, and if it's meat, I thank the animal for their sacrifice to feed me and allow me to live because of them, and I wish them a more fortunate rebirth.

If you accidentally step on a bug and kill it, you should pray for it and wish it a fortunate rebirth. Likewise, you would do the same for the meat you're about to eat.

I was wondering if it were possible to study Buddhism and participate and identify as a Buddhist while still believing in God and Christianity. Do you know anything about this?

My personal opinions about mixing religions differ slightly of what many others would probably say. Personally and many Buddhists would say, you can't *be* Buddhist and Christian, but you can *practice* Buddhism and be Christian.

Buddhism is not so much a religion as it is a philosophy of a better way of living. Because it does not have a belief in a god or a creator, it contradicts being a Christian. So how can you be with a non-god believing religion and also a god-believing religion at the same time? You contradict yourself and your beliefs.

On the other hand, taking away the "religious" part of Buddhism and practicing its core practices (compassion, generosity, kindness, morality, non-discrimination, non-violence, etc.) in conjunction with your religion, is perfectly acceptable and practiced by a lot of non-Buddhists. It makes you a better practitioner of your own religion.

At my temple, 90% of new visitors are Christian/Catholic and come to study and practice meditation and the basics of Buddhism to add to their own practices of their religion. They know with a little more help from outside their religion can help their personal goals and lives.

Ultimately, religion is a personal practice. No one can tell you what's right or wrong except you. The Buddha said, "Out of respect for me, just because I am the Buddha do not believe everything I say. Take what I have said and practice it, contemplate on it – does it make sense or not?" So it's up to you to take the teachings of your own religion and Buddhism's and figure out, through meditation and contemplation, what does and doesn't make sense, what you believe and don't believe – then, you have your religion.

Part X

Miscellaneous

How Do Buddhists Pray?

Prayer comes in all shapes, sizes, and forms, and it's part of every major religion's practices. But prayer in Buddhism is much different. Because Buddhism is nontheistic, it is a mind-centered religion, so there's not anything or anyone that Buddhists pray to. Though depending on the school of Buddhism and the country Buddhism is in, prayer is sometimes directed to a certain Buddha or Bodhisattva asking for help or guidance.

Actual prayer in Buddhism is very different than prayer in other major religions. Prayer in Buddhism should only be directed to ourselves. Because Buddhism is a self-liberating path, Buddhists can't rely on anyone or anything for enlightenment, just ourselves. Prayer should not have any "wants" or "needs." Instead, prayer should be a self-reminder of what we're praying for. If we're trying to cultivate compassion, we should pray for the courage and dedication it takes to cultivate and generate

237

compassion in a chaotic society. Not praying to anyone, but praying to ourselves to remind and encourage ourselves to hold on to compassion even in the most difficult of times.

In some Asian countries, we will see statues of Avalokitesvara with a sign saying "The Wish-Fulfilling Bodhisattva." This is very incorrect. The Buddha had said many times that if we wanted something, only we can create the causes and conditions to obtain it. We can't be praying to Avalokitesvara saying, "Avalokitesvara bodhisattva, please help me get money... help me get well... help me with the courage to ask this girl out." No! Avalokitesvara Bodhisattva is not there to help us get rich, get laid and magically get well! That's not how it works.

In prayer, in any religion, should not be for asking for something. That defeats the purpose of prayer. Prayer should be the means of helping ourselves concentrate on something so we can find the solution ourselves. Why would we ask God, Buddha, or a bodhisattva for money if all we're doing is sitting on the couch watching TV or playing video games? Like everything else in life, we must apply *effort* and *dedication* so we can achieve what we want. Like a job interview, we can't just go in and "wing it." That's definitely NOT going to get us the job. Instead, we must research the job description, the company, the benefits, etc. if we want to impress the interviewer. There is work involved to get the job to give us work!

We cannot have blind faith and pray to anything or anyone for something we want. That just makes us lazy. If we want something but put no work into making it happen, then we're lazy, and we will never accomplish anything.

So Buddhist prayer is about reminding ourselves to cultivate the characteristic we want. If we pray to a Bodhisattva, each bodhisattva has a specific attribute that we can pray for. Avalokitesvara, the bodhisattva of compassion - we pray for the ability to cultivate and practice compassion in difficult times. Manjushri, the bodhisattva of great wisdom - we pray that our practice will gain us great wisdom towards our enlightenment. Ksitigarbha, the bodhisattva that saves beings from hell, we pray that we will have the courage and ability to save people from their own demons and difficult times. This is Buddhist prayer.

Why do Buddhists chant sutras?

Way back when, in the olden days of the Buddha, all of Buddha's teachings were passed down orally. Nothing was written down until a few hundred years after Buddha's passing away. So memorizing and chanting the sutras was the only way to preserve and teach the Dharma. The same way we might not be able to remember a speech just by listening to it once, nor did the people back then either.

Even though we've had the sutras in written form for the past two thousand years now, sutras are still chanted. Chanting is a form of meditation. When a text is chanted, we are better able to concentrate on just the text and better understand it versus just reading it. Just like a song that's memorized after listening to it a dozen times, a sutra (depending on its length) can also be memorized after a dozen or two times of chanting. When it's memorized, we can then put more focus on understanding the meaning behind the message of the sutra, instead of trying to recall the words.

__What is your opinion on the different schools of Buddhism? Do you believe that there's right and wrong? I'm really conflicted and worry if I'm following the right path. I've heard criticism of each school of Buddhism, so I am truly confused as to what I should follow.__

Just like every other religion, they each have their different traditions, congregations, sects, etc. Each competes with the other to be the "right" and "only" religion. But in Buddhism, we have many traditions and schools because it had to adapt to the culture and society it was being introduced to.

Regardless of the different schools, sects, paths, and traditions of Buddhism, they all have the same, basic teachings of the Buddha (Four Noble Truths, Eightfold Path, meditation, etc.). There are some schools and traditions that emphasize certain teachings over others like Zen with meditation, or schools like Tiantai that primarily works with and emphasizes the Lotus Sutra or the Pure Land school of Amitabha.

Regardless of what criticism there are for any of the schools or traditions, the decision is ultimately up to us. We have to find what works for us, what agrees with us, and ultimately what will liberate us. We can even go rogue and study sutras and texts based on our own interest and beliefs. No person, school, or tradition can enlighten us; only *we* can enlighten ourselves! The teachings are simply the tools and guides to help us get there, but only we can be the captain of our ship to cross from the shore of suffering.

Do you know anything about the OM symbol and what it means? I heard things like it's the sound of the universe and that it represents the unison of the

body and mind, but I'm still confused. Could you clarify maybe?

That pretty much covers the basics. There are three root sounds of the universe: OM AH HUM. Om is the first and most important. It is the mother of all sounds, the most important sound, it is the ocean of breath. Sometimes in Esoteric Buddhism, they just chant one sound: om om om.

Om also symbolizes our impure body, speech and mind, and that it can lead us to the Truth and have the pure, exalted body, speech, and mind of a Buddha. Symbolically, it also means to "listen," because what follows is important and should be heard/read.

Can you briefly describe the difference between the types of Buddhism?

There are two "types" or major schools of Buddhism: Mahayana and Theravada (or Hinayana).

Theravada is practiced in many Southeast Asian countries and of course around the world. Theravadans only practice the teachings and meditations that came directly from our historical Buddha Sakyamuni. In Theravada, the highest accomplishment is reaching Nirvana or Arahatship, but only for those that live a monastic life.

Mahayana has many schools under its umbrella like Vajrayana (Tibetan Buddhism), Zen and Pure Land. Unlike Theravada, Mahayana incorporates many other Buddhas and Bodhisattvas (saints) into its practice; giving people more ways to practice according to their suits and needs to reach enlightenment. In Mahayana, the highest accomplishment is reaching Buddhahood! In Mahayana, everyone – lay people and monastics, have the capability to become a Buddha.

Most Buddhist temples and centers in the West are either of Tibetan Buddhism, Chinese/Zen, or Thai.

Neither major school is better than the other. Both have the same ultimate aspiration: to eradicate suffering/dissatisfaction. It's up to the practitioner to find the school/tradition that suits their needs and beliefs.

Do you recommend looking at Buddhist art as a way to be able to learn more about Buddhism? Like does art teach you about it in ways that words can't?

Isn't that how we've learned a great chunk of history, through art? Buddhist art is absolutely gorgeous. Even Christian art is breath-taking. But since art is a "thing," it can only go so far to teach us anything. Just like words can only describe something so much before words run out.

The same goes for our Buddha Nature or emptiness; it can't be described with words. It's something we must discover and realize on our own. So when we interpret art, architecture, nature, history, people, colors, foods, etc. what we can learn from them is limited. Whether based on our intelligence, interpretation, vocabulary, or anything else.

If I tried to write down my own description and interpretation of a piece of Buddhist art for you and you for me, we would most likely come up with some big differences. So who's right? Who's interpretation of this piece of history is correct?

Anyway, art can teach us a lot of valuable information. That's why we go to museums; not just to stare blindly at the exhibits, but to learn from them and gain some knowledge we've never had before.

Can you expand on what a hungry ghost is?

The image of a hungry ghost in Buddhist literature and art is of a greedy person with a big belly and a long, narrow neck. Every time they try to eat something, it turns into fire, and they're not able to eat it.

One of my favorite stories of a hungry ghost is of Maudgalyayana's mother. She was a cruel and greedy woman in her life. She always mocked and slandered the Dharma. When monks would go out for alms, she would give them dog meat. Her cruelty and greediness lead her to hell. When Maudgalayayana became an Arhat, he obtained supernatural powers and used them to see where his mother was.

When he saw her in hell, he transformed himself there and tried to offer her a bowl of rice. Because of her greediness, she took the bowl of rice with one hand and used the other hand to hide the bowl from the other hungry ghosts so she wouldn't have to share. But she couldn't eat it because the bowl of rice turned into fire. Maudgalayayana was sad and cried for his mother.

He then went to the Buddha and told him what he had seen and asked what he could do. The Buddha told him to take 99 other monks and him to make 100 and pray for her.

Eventually, the mother heard her son's prayers, and she vowed to be a better person, and she was reborn out of hell.

In the real world, a "hungry ghost" represents people who are by nature selfish, greedy in helping others, avaricious, angry, full of desires and ignorance. They are the people who are constantly after things and always wanting more, never believing they have enough. Though a hungry ghost is one of the three unfortunate ways of rebirth, they can still be successful and wealthy people, but whom are deeply suffering and dissatisfied.

To avoid rebirth as a hungry ghost, we practice compassion and generosity.

I have a question about all the different forms of Buddhism there are: it's pretty overwhelming, to say the least.
I've been reading a lot, A LOT, because I want to be open to all forms and not just think, eh, that's the most popular one, let's pick that one. Doesn't work that way obviously. Anyhow, despite all my study into this subject I still feel kind of lost. Of course, I could visit a temple, but still, too many choices! For me, at this moment, it feels like all forms, whether it's Zen, Pure Land, Nichiren, etc., etc., all have something that feels like; oh, this feels good! Maybe I'm too focused on choosing, I know, but in a way I think I'll feel more grounded, for lack of a better word, if I choose one. Any advice?

That is an excellent question!

Yes, there are a LOT of choices out there, and they're there to suit the needs of every kind of person and their needs.

Depending on where you live, choosing a temple and teacher is either easy or difficult, whether it's because you have many options or no options at all. Every temple and teacher's teaching style and path that they're trying to lead the people with are different.

Despite the many choices, all schools and traditions still teach and emphasize the basic core of Buddhist teachings: Four Noble Truths, Eightfold path, meditation, karma, compassion, non-violence, equanimity, and the end of suffering.

There are so many choices to choose from because so many people learn in different ways. You might be a visual learner whereas I have to actually do the work and practice. So two different teaching methods need to be created.

There are two ways to "choose" a school/tradition. 1) You can sit down and contemplate what it is you want to learn and achieve. Are there certain teachings/sutras you want to master? Are you trying to achieve high levels of meditation? Do you want a helping hand and an easy route out of suffering into a Pure Land? Think of what you want to be learning and how you want to be learning it.

2) You can just let it fall into your lap. For years, I lived about eight minutes from my temple that I never knew existed. At the time, I was only self-studying and hadn't made the choice to go to/join a temple yet. When I finally did make the choice, I was surprised that there was one right down the road from me! Not only that, but

there was another temple even closer, but something drew me to the one I started going to. It kind of just happened.

There aren't many temple choices around here, so the one I did decide to go to, I have a very strong connection to. I didn't seek a certain tradition or school; I just let it come to me. So if you have many options, great! Visit each one for a month or so to really gauge its atmosphere, teachings, and people, and that should help you make a choice. Or you can visit one of them and instantly know, "This is the one!"

Or, if all else fails – You don't really need a tradition/school. As long as you're practicing the basics and live with morality, then that's all the tradition you need. If you do self-study, pick one or two sutras that you feel a real connection to and stick to those sutras and study them for the rest of your life. That becomes your tradition.

I am starting to practice Buddhism. Someone in my family is very close to me, but they always seem to want to make me jealous of them in some way. I think it's because they are insecure and in some way jealous of me. Since I realize this, I try not to get upset about it, but it's difficult to stay positive

***when you're being attacked all the time. I've
meditated on this too, and I've tried to respond
positively to these negative feelings, but it doesn't
seem to be helping. Do you have any tips?***

I'm glad you've started your practice and are
practicing controlling negative feelings. A lot of people
come to Buddhism "knowing" it's this positive, peaceful,
always happy, tree-hugging religion, and not really
understanding the true concepts of Buddhism. Buddhism
is not a fix to our problems. It's not a medicine that'll
solve all our issues overnight. Buddhism is a guide to
lead us to a way to solve our problems; it is not the
antidote, it is the ingredients for us to create the antidote.

We have to treat everyone who may cause neutral or
negative thoughts like children, and we are the parents –
it doesn't matter who, what, how old, or what their
religion is. Because as children we learn from what we
see our parents doing, including the way they say things,
do things, handle certain situations or people, their
behavior, etc. If we grow up with kind, patient parents,
we will (hopefully) also inherit those qualities. But if we
grow up with angry, unkind parents, then we will also
have those qualities.

Likewise, even though your family members are of
course not your children, but continuing to stay and say
positive things will only do good. After a while, and it
could be a long while, they will start to see the change in

you and how you react to things, but will hopefully spark something in them to come to that realization and follow in your path.

We all have positive, negative and neutral seeds in our consciousness – it just takes certain circumstances and conditions for those seeds to grow. Some of us have more growing negative seeds than positive, others with more positive – but all have equal opportunities to grow and flourish, it's your job to water the seeds you wish to bloom.

So continue what you're doing. Continue staying and being positive and watering your positive seeds. Their negativity cannot hurt you unless you allow it to. Otherwise, it is just empty words that make them sound like fools because they see that it doesn't affect you.

What can you tell me regarding the literal aspect of the six realms? Some say they're states of mind, some say literal places. How do you see it?

They're a little bit of both; I think (believe).

So we have the three "fortunate" realms: human, asura ("demi-gods") and deva ("heavenly beings"). Human is obvious so that I won't go into that. Asuras are portrayed as beings addicted to passion, pride, and envy. They are beings that have the means and the intentions of doing good, but end up committing bad actions and harming others. In a modern and real sense, Asuras are people who may be wealthy or in politics that do not contribute positively to the people and society. They are privileged people that go after power and control and do not stop for more.

Devas, on the other hand, are pretty much the opposite of Asuras. They are generally happier, more peaceful, longer living beings. In human form, they also could be wealthy or privileged people, but do not share the negative characteristics of Asuras. Instead, they are generous, compassionate and kind people who share their wealth or success with others.

Then we have the three "unfortunate" realms: hell, hungry ghosts, and animals. Animals could be taken both literally and figuratively because obviously there are real animals (some who act or think they're human!), and then there are people who act like animals (with violence, anger, killing, etc.). To be reborn as an animal are people who were violent towards people and animals, harness anger and ignorance, and those with false views (i.e. believe that their truth is the absolute truth, even when it's wrong).

Likewise, hell could also be taken literally or figuratively. At one point or another, we might all feel like we live in hell or a hellish place. Our lives seem completely useless, everything is going wrong, nothing is in our favor, we constantly want more but can never have, etc. Hell is also a state of mind when we get so overwhelmed with anger and hate, that everything within and around us is chaotic. Beings reborn in hell are those who were greedy, selfish, ignorant, and those who feel that giving charity or donations is the hardest thing in the world.

When we see Buddhist art or images of hell beings, they are depicted as people with big bellies and a long, narrow neck, and whenever they try to eat or drink something, it turns into flames and burns them. Because they were greedy and never wanted to give in their past lives, now they will not be able to get anything either.

What is Pure Land and Zen Buddhism?

Briefly, Pure Land and Zen Buddhism are two of the largest schools of Mahayana Buddhism. Each originated in India and was brought to China and then later spread all over Asia.

Pure Land Buddhism focuses on Amitabha (or Amitayus) Buddha who resides in his Land of Bliss called Sukhavati. Amitabha Buddha made 48 vows to save all sentient beings and accepts all into his Pure Land for those who have faith in and recite his name with sincerity.

Pure Land Buddhism has three main sutras:
The Shorter Sukhavativyuha Sutra (Amitabha Sutra),
Longer Sukhavativyuha Sutra (Infinite Life Sutra), and
the Amitayurdhyana Sutra (Amitayus Meditation Sutra).

Statues of Amitabha will almost always also have
the Bodhisattvas Avalokitesvara to his right and
Mahasthamaprapta to his left that help aid the dying
person to the Pure Land.

The Indian monk, Bodhidharma, brought Zen to
China (Chán Buddhism). Zen has many different schools
and traditions, but they all emphasize a rigorous
meditation practice. Unlike other Buddhist schools, Zen
doesn't emphasize practice and teaching through sutras,
but through direct transmission from an accomplished
teacher through zazen meditation.

However, Zen services do have chanting.
The Tathagatagarbha Sutras, Prajnaparamita collections,
the Heart Sutra, Great Compassion mantra and some
other lesser mantras are some of the most important text.

Sharing the Merit

Whatever virtue and benefit accomplished that may come from this book, I transfer the merit to all sentient beings so that they may accomplish full enlightenment.

May the roots of suffering and their causes be free from all sentient beings.

May the roots of ignorance and their causes be free from all sentient beings.

May the roots of greed and their causes be free from all sentient beings.

May the roots of anger and their causes be free from all sentient beings.

May all sentient beings be free from violence, poor health, neglect, indifference, and addiction.

May all sentient beings gain great wisdom and compassion.

May we continue to open our hearts and our minds for the benefit of all beings.

May we cross the ocean of suffering and delight together to the shore of enlightenment.

Chants and Prayers

Six-Syllable Mantra

The six-syllable mantra is probably one of the most popular mantras amongst Buddhists. It is the mantra of *Karuna*, or compassion, associated with the Bodhisattva *Avalokitesvara*. The direct translation of the mantra is "The Jewel in the Lotus."

The mantra is believed to cover all Buddhist sutras, Shastras (commentary of scriptures), and Vinaya. Basically, it covers all the literature in Buddhism. In some traditions, Om Mani Padme Hum covers and is equal to all other mantras because it is equal to the same meaning and merit to all those mantras.

Om is the sound of the universe, the mother of all sounds, and the most important sound. It also represents our impure body, speech, and mind and it can lead us to the Truth and have the pure, exalted body, speech, and mind of a Buddha. Symbolically, om means to "listen," because what follows is important and should be heard/read carefully.

Mani is the essence, the reality, the core of everything. It's the Buddha Nature in ourselves.

Padme is the functionality and merits – purification, pacification, understanding the mind through meditation, through chanting, repentance, through all the good deeds we've done, good behavior, and our speech; we're carrying out Padme.

Hum is in every aspect of life: what we've done, what we're doing, what we've spoken, what we're about to speak. It's a method and approach to Enlightenment. It's the three elements in everything: the essence, the form, and the function.

OM MANI PADME HUM

Mantra Of Shakyamuni Buddha

The mantra of Sakyamuni Buddha is a simple mantra that can be chanted anywhere and everywhere. It is a mantra of concentration, courage, and wisdom.

OM MUNI MUNI MAHAMUNI SHAKYAMUNI SVAHA

Mantra Of Medicine Buddha

In the *Bhaiṣajyaguruvaiḍūryaprabhārāja Sūtra*, the Medicine Buddha is described as having entered into a state of samadhi called "Eliminating All the Suffering and Afflictions of Sentient Beings." From this samadhi state, he spoke the Medicine Buddha Dharani.

NAMO BHAGAVATE BHAIṢAJYAGURU VAIḌŪRYAPRABHARĀJĀYA TATHĀGATĀYA ARHATE SAMYAKSAMBUDDHĀYA TADYATHĀ: OṂ BHAIṢAJYE BHAIṢAJYE MAHĀBHAIṢAJYA-SAMUDGATE SVĀHĀ.

The last line of the Dharani is used as Bhaisajyaguru's short form mantra.

Mantra Of Amitabha Buddha

Just like reciting the Sutra of Amitabha Buddha, reciting Amitabha's name, or mantra, 108 times with sincere understanding ensures a rebirth in Amitabha's Pure Land.

OṂ AMIDEVA HRĪḤ

Great Compassion Mantra

This Sanskrit version of The Great Compassion Mantra, Nilakantha Dharani or Mahakaruna Dharani, is a popular mantra also associated with the Bodhisattva Avalokitesvara. Chanted for protection and purification.

1. Namo ratna-trayāya
2. Namo āriyā
3. Valokite-śvarāya
4. Bodhi-sattvāya
5. Maha-sattvāya
6. Mahā-kārunikāya
7. Om
8. Sarva-raviye
9. Sudhanadasya
10. Namo skritvā imam āryā
11. Valokite-śvara Randhawa
12. Namo narakindi
13. Hrih Mahā-vat-svāme
14. Sarva-arthato-śubham
15. Ajeyam
16. Sarva-satva Namo-vasatva Namo-vāka
17. Mavitāto
18. Tadyathā
19. Om avaloki
20. Lokate
21. Krate

22. E Hrih
23. Mahā-bodhisattva
24. Sarva sarva
25. Mala mala
26. Mahi Mahi ridayam
27. Kuru kuru karmam
28. Dhuru dhuru vijayate
29. Mahā-vijayati
30. Dhara dhara
31. Dhrini
32. Śvarāya
33. Chala chala
34. Mama vimala
35. Muktele
36. Ehi ehi
37. Śhina śhina
38. Ārsam prasari
39. Viśva viśvam
40. Prasaya
41. Hulu hulu mara
42. Hulu hulu hrih
43. Sara sara
44. Siri siri
45. Suru suru
46. Bodhiya Bodhiya
47. Bodhaya Bodhaya
48. Maitreya
49. Narakindi

50. Dhrish-nina
51. Bhayamana
52. Svāhā
53. Siddhāya
54. Svāhā
55. Maha siddhāya
56. Svāhā
57. Siddha-yoge
58. Śvaraya
59. Svāhā
60. Narakindi
61. Svāhā
62. Māranara
63. Svāhā
64. Śira simha-mukhāya
65. Svāhā
66. Sarva mahā-asiddhaya
67. Svāhā
68. Cakra-asiddhāya
69. Svāhā
70. Padma-kastāya
71. Svāhā
72. Narakindi-vagalāya
73. Svaha
74. Mavari-śankharāya
75. Svāhā
76. Namo ratna-trāyāya
77. Namo āryā

78. Valokite
79. Śvaraya
80. Svāhā
81. Om Sidhyantu
82. Mantra
83. Padāya
84. Svāhā

Great Compassion Mantra
Alternative Version

1. Namo Ratnatrayaya
2. Namo Arya
3. Avalokiteshavaraya
4. Bodhisattvaya
5. Mahasattvaya
6. Mahakarunikaya
7. Om
8. Savalavati
9. Sudhanatasya
10. Namaskrittva Naman Arya
11. Avalokiteshavara Lantabha
12. Namo Nilakantha
13. Srimahapatashami
14. Sarvadvatashubham
15. Ashiyum

16. Sarvasattva Namo Pasattva Namo Bhaga
17. Ma-Bhate-Tu
18. Tadyatha
19. Om! Avaloka
20. Lokate
21. Kalati
22. Ishiri
23. Mahabodhisattva
24. Sabho Sabho
25. Mara Mara
26. Mashi Mashi Ridhayu
27. Guru Guru Ghamain
28. Dhuru Dhuru Bhashiyati
29. Maha Bhashiyati
30. Dhara Dhara
31. Dhirini
32. Shvaraya
33. Jala Jala
34. Mahabhamara
35. Mudhill
36. E-Hy-Ehi
37. Shina Shina
38. Alashinbalashari
39. Basha Bhasnin
40. Bharashaya
41. Huluhulu Pra
42. Hulu Hulu Shri
43. Sara Sara

44. Siri Siri

45. Suru Suru

46. Buddhaya Buddhaya

47. Bodhaya Bodhaya

48. Maitriye

49. Nilakansta

50. Trisa Rana

51. Bhaya Mane

52. Svaha

53. Sitaya

54. Svaha

55. Maha Sitaya

56. Svaha

57. Sitayaye

58. Svaraya

59. Svaha

60. Nilakanthi

61. Svaha

62. Pranila

63. Svaha

64. Shrisimhamukhaya

65. Svaha

66. Sarvamahasastaya

67. Svaha

68. Chakra Astaya

69. Svaha

70. Padmakesshaya

71. Svaha

72. Nilakantepantalaya
73. Svaha
74. Mopholishankaraya
75. Svaha
76. Namo Ratnatrayaya
77. Namo Arya
78. Avalokite
79. Shavaraya
80. Svaha
81. Om! Siddhyantu
82. Mantra
83. Pataya
84. Svaha

Prayer Of The Awakening Mind

With the wish to free all beings
I shall always take refuge
In the Buddha, Dharma, and Sangha,
Until the attainment of full enlightenment.

Enthused by compassion and wisdom,
Today in the Buddha's presence
I generate the mind for full awakening
For the benefit of all beings.

As long as space remains,
As long as sentient beings remain,
May I too remain
And dispel the miseries of the world!

Mantra Of Prajnaparamita

The Prajnaparamita mantra is found at the end of the classical Buddhist scripture *The Heart of Prajnaparamita Sutra* or often called *The Heart Sutra* or *The Heart of Perfect Understanding Sutra*.

There are many different translations of this mantra, but all are fairly similar and give the same basic concept. Prajna means 'wisdom.' Paramita has many meanings depending on the context, but here it means 'crossing all the way over' or 'going beyond.' Therefore, the mantra can be translated to be: "Gone, gone, gone all the way over, gone with all beings to the other shore. Enlightenment, rejoice!"

We cross the sea of suffering, our dissatisfied lives, to the shore of liberation. Buddha gave us a raft, the Dharma, to use to cross this sea of suffering to the shore of enlightenment. Once in the raft, we must use effort and have confidence that we will reach the shore, avoiding the thrashing of the waves trying to push us back into the water. (hint: Gate is pronounced as "gah-tay").

GATE GATE PARAGATE PARASAMGATE BODHI SVAHA

Prayer For Repentance

As ordinary human beings, we are still not perfect, we are not yet a Buddha. We still hold ignorance, delusion, anger, jealousy, and greed. We can commit and accumulate bad karma every day, no matter how subtle the thought, speech, or action is. So we repent. We don't repent and expect our negative karma to disappear or be blessed by the Buddha or Bodhisattvas. We repent as a means of promising ourselves to never do it again. In front of an image of the Buddha or Bodhisattva we make this promise three or more times every day:

FOR ANY MISDEEDS I HAVE CAUSED BY MY MIND, SPEECH, OR ACTION DUE TO MY IGNORANCE, GREED, AND ANGER, I REPENT.

Taking Refuge In The Triple Gem

I take refuge in the Buddha,
The fully Enlightened one,
The one who shows me the way to awakening.

I take refuge in the Dharma,
The way to achieve my awakening.

I take refuge in the Sangha,
The community that helps me achieve my awakening.

Homage To The Buddha And Bodhisattvas

Homage to Sakaymuni Buddha, the fully enlightened one, to whom we bow in gratitude.
Homage to Avaloketisvara, Great Compassion Bodhisattva.
Homage to Manjushri, Great Wisdom Bodhisattva.
Homage to Samantabahdara, Great Action Bodhisattva.
Homage to Kshitigarbha, Great Aspiration Bodhisattva.
Homage to Maitreya, the Buddha to-be-born.
Homage to all Buddhas and Bodhisattvas to whom we bow in gratitude.

269

Buddhist Glossary

Ananda: One of Sakyamuni Buddha's Ten Great Disciples, and the Buddha's cousin. He was first in hearing the Buddha's words. He had a photographic memory, so he memorized the Buddha's sermons, which were later recorded as sutras.

Anapanasati: Mindful breathing meditation.

Arhat: lit. "the Worthy One," a living person who has reached Enlightenment.

Asura: Demi-gods of the desire realm are called Asuras. A race of beings who, like the Titans of Greek mythology, fought the devas for sovereignty over the heavens and lost. Asuras populate one of the six realms of samsara. Asuras are typically depicted as titans or warrior beings.

Atman: literally "self," sometimes "soul" or "ego." In Buddhism, the predominant teaching is the negating doctrine of anatman, that there is no permanent, persisting atman, and that belief in atman is the prime consequence of ignorance, the foundation of samsara.

Attachment: A deluded mental factor or perception that observes a person or object and regards it as a cause or source of lasting happiness.

Avalokitesvara: lit. "One Who Hears the Suffering Cries of the World," The bodhisattva of compassion. Also see

271

Guan Yin.

Awakening: Spiritual realization; complete purity and wisdom. The ultimate goal of Buddhist practice. Full liberation from ignorance and suffering. Purified of all obscurations, defilements, and misperceptions of reality. The development of all perfect qualities and wisdom. Also, see *Enlightenment.*

Bodhi: Awakening or Enlightenment.

Bodhi Tree: The Sacred Fig (*Ficus religiosa*) tree under which Gautama reached Enlightenment.

Bodhichitta: The awakened heart-mind of love, wisdom, and compassion. Mind of enlightenment. *Bodhi* means enlightenment, and *Chitta* means mind. Generally speaking, the term 'bodhichitta' refers to the mind which is motivated by the great compassion that spontaneously seeks enlightenment to benefit all living beings.

Bodhisattva: One with the intention to become a Buddha in order to liberate all other sentient beings from suffering.

Bodhisattva-mahasattva: The suffix mahasattva ('Great Being') signifies a bodhisattva who's awakening is very advanced, approaching that of a Buddha.

Buddha: The fully awakened/enlightened one.

Buddhahood: See *Enlightenment.*

Buddha nature: The uncreated and deathless Buddhic

272

element or principle concealed within all sentient beings to achieve Awakening; the innate (latent) Buddha essence
(especially in the Tathagatagarbha sutras, Tendai/Tiantai, Nichiren thought).

Buddhism: The teachings of the historical Buddha, Siddhartha Gautama, are the basis of what is called Buddhism. Buddhism can be subdivided into Hiniyana (the Lesser Vehicle), Mahayana (the Great Vehicle), and Vajrayana (The Diamond Way).

Buddhist: Anyone who from the depths of their heart goes for refuge to the Three Jewels—Buddha, Dharma, and Sangha.

Buddho: Awake; enlightened. An epithet for the Buddha.

Chakra / Cakra (Sanskrit): Dharma wheel. Energy centers located along the spinal column in the subtle body, having a direct relationship to the endocrine glands of the physical body.

Citta: Mind; heart; state of consciousness.

Compassion: The mind that cannot bear the suffering of others and wishes them to be free from it. To vibrate in sympathy with others. True compassion is guided by wisdom and love, not emotional reaction and pity.

Cyclic Existence: The cycle of death and rebirth, which is influenced by the power of delusion and karma. The

273

cycle of death and rebirth is fraught with the dissatisfaction and suffering which arises from ignorance of the true nature of reality. Also see *Samsara*.

Dana: Generosity or giving; in Buddhism, it also refers to the practice of cultivating generosity. The first of the Six Paramitas.

Dependent Origination: The principal that nothing exists independently, but comes into existence only in dependence upon various previous causes and conditions. There are twelve successive phases of this process that begin with ignorance and end with old age and death.

Desire Realm: One of the three realms of cyclic existence mentioned in Buddhist scriptures. This is a realm where beings enjoy five external sense objects: form, sound, smell, touch, and taste. There are six realms within this desire realm: god (deva), demigod (asura), and human, which are the happy or higher realms, and the animal, hungry ghost, and hell realms, which are the unhappy or lower realms.

Deva: Literally, "shining one." An inhabitant of the heavenly realms.

Devadatta: A cousin of the Buddha who tried to effect a schism in the sangha and who has since become emblematic for all Buddhists who work knowingly or unknowingly to undermine the religion from within.

Dharani (Sanskrit): A formula said to protect one who

recites it. Also said to benefit one's progress towards awakening by virtue of its mystical power. The word Dharani literally means "to preserve and uphold" the Buddha's teachings in one's heart. Dharanis are recited in Sanskrit and sometimes have no literal meaning. They are especially valued in esoteric Buddhism.

Dharma (Sanskrit) / **Dhamma** (Pali): The word "dharma" derives from the Sanskrit "dhri" which means to preserve, maintain, keep, uphold. "Dharma" has a great variety of meanings, including law, truth, doctrine, the Buddha's teaching, steadfast decree, customary observance, prescribed conduct, duty, virtue, morality, good deeds, religion, justice, nature, quality, character, characteristic, essential quality, elements of existence, ultimate constituents of things. "Dharma" also refers to that which subsists; event, a phenomenon in and of itself; principles of behavior that human beings should follow so as to be in accordance with the right and natural order of reality; righteous living. Dharma is the underlying meaning of the Buddha's teachings; that truth upon which all Buddhist practices, scriptures, and philosophy have as a foundation.

Dharma Wheel: The "Dharma Wheel" or "Wheel of Dharma" is a metaphor for the unfolding and maturation of the Dharma in the world, once it has been revealed by a Buddha. 'Setting the Dharma Wheel in motion' is another way of saying revealing and propagating the Dharma. Also known as *dharmachakra.*

275

Dhyana (Sanskrit): Meditation; concentration. The practice of focusing the mind on one point in order to purify one's heart, eradicate illusions and perceive the ultimate truth. Practiced widely in India before Sakyamuni, meditation acquired new significance as the fifth of the six paramitas in Buddhism. In China, the Ch'an (Zen) school was established with meditation as its sole practice for attaining enlightenment. Dhyana is the Sanskrit word of which Ch'an and Zen are Chinese and Japanese transliterations.

Dukkha: Suffering, dissatisfaction.

Eightfold Path / Noble Eightfold Path: The Eightfold Path offered by Sakyamuni Buddha whereby one may achieve liberation from suffering and attain full awakening. Eight factors of spiritual practice leading to the extinction of suffering: Right Understanding, Right Thought, Right Speech, Right Action, Right Livelihood, Right Effort, Right Mindfulness, Right Concentration. It is important to realize that no matter how profound one's conceptual knowledge of this Path may be, this will not be sufficient for true accomplishment. It is essential that one follows, cultivates, and practices this Noble Path with diligence, sincerity, and full confidence.

Eight Worldly (Mundane) Concerns: The eight mundane concerns arise in connection with worldly or material life, they are: Gain and loss, honor and dishonor, happiness and misery, praise and blame.

Emptiness: Shunyata (Sanskrit), Sunyata (Pali). A

description of enlightenment. The ultimate nature of all phenomena. The actual way in which all things exist. To the western mind, the idea of Emptiness is often difficult to understand, leading to the notion that it is 'nothing,' and therefore quite unattractive. However, emptiness can be understood as the Buddhist way of saying that Ultimate Reality is incapable of being described, much the way that Christian theologians view God as beyond human description. Emptiness should not be thought of as another location. Instead, it is identical to the world or universe humans experience in this life. In this way, it is much like the Hindu notion that this world is simply Maya (illusion), which prevents humans from seeing the true unity of the cosmos (which in Hinduism means the identity of Atman and Brahman, the True Self, god is everything and everyone). Thus, Emptiness and the phenomena of this world are the same. As the Heart Sutra says, "form is emptiness, emptiness is form."

Enlightenment: The full enlightenment of Buddhahood. Awakening. Enlightenment is the full liberation from and a true cessation of ignorance and suffering. Enlightenment or Buddhahood is a state of complete purity and wisdom.

Equanimity: An impartial and imperturbable composure of heart. A love that embraces all living beings and circumstances with equality, wisdom, and complete serenity. With this sublime quality of equanimity our love is impartial, rightly discerning, balanced, not carried away by emotion, and free of attachment. Equanimity is the essential foundation on which one develops the compassionate motivation of a Bodhisattva.

Five Precepts or Five Training Rules: The five basic guidelines for training oneself in wholesome actions of body and speech: (1) refraining from killing other beings; (2) refraining from stealing; (3) refraining from sexual misconduct; (4) refraining from lying and false speech; (5) refraining from using intoxicants that cloud the mind.

Formless Realm: In this realm, which is further beyond the desire realm than the form realm, beings have renounced form and exist only within the stream of consciousness. Although they have temporarily abandoned attachment to form pleasures, their minds are still bound by subtle desire and attachment to mental states and ego. Therefore, this formless realm is still within samsara (cyclic existence).

Form Realm: One of the three realms of cyclic existence beyond the desire realm. Here beings have renounced the enjoyment of external sense objects, yet still have an attachment to internal form, that is, their own body and mind.

Four Noble Truths: The fundamental doctrine of Sakyamuni Buddha, the foundation of all Dharma teachings. 1) The Truth of Suffering and Dissatisfaction. 2) The Truth of the Origin of Suffering and Dissatisfaction. 3) The Truth of the Ending of Suffering and Dissatisfaction. 4) The Truth of the Path Leading to End of Suffering and Dissatisfaction (The Noble

Eightfold Path).

God Realm: There are three god realms of various kinds, one is in the desire realm, the other two are in the form and formless realms. Also known as the realm of Devas.

Guan Yin: The bodhisattva of compassion in East Asian Buddhism, with full name being Guan Shi Yin. Guan Yin is considered to be the female form of Avalokitesvara but has been given many more distinctive characteristics.

Hell Realm: The lowest of the realms within the desire realm.

Higher Realms: The god (Deva), demigod (Asura), and human realms, which are all part of cyclic existence or samsara.

Hum or Hung: A mantra or mantric syllable regarded as the 'Essence of all Buddhas' (vajra spirit). The non-dual wisdom of the Buddhas. Hum/Hung symbolizes the integration of the universal/absolute into the individual. It is the inseparability of emptiness and bliss. Hum/Hung is often used at the end of mantras as the spiritual achievement of one's intentions, bringing the absolute into form; corresponding in a certain way to the word Amen of the Christian. Hum/Hung is associated with the heart center and the color deep blue. Practice with this mantra dissolves harmful and disturbing thoughts and feelings and brings spontaneous joy.

Insight Meditation (Sanskrit: <u>Vipassana</u>): Meditation that develops insight into the nature of mind. The other main meditation is samatha meditation. Also see *Vipassana*.

Kalpa: A vast expanse of time; an eon. In Indian creation mythology, the duration of the world consists of four asankhya kalpas, during which the world arises, subsists, decays, and is destroyed. Then, the cycle is renewed.

Karma: lit. "action," The law of cause and effect in Buddhism.

Karuṇā: Compassion; sympathy; the aspiration to find a way to be truly helpful to oneself and others. One of the Six Paramitas (perfections).

Koan: A story, question, problem or statement generally inaccessible to rational understanding, yet may be accessible to Intuition.

Law of Causal Condition: The fundamental doctrine of Buddhism that all phenomena in the universe are produced by causation. Since all phenomena result from the complicated causes and effects, all existing things in the universe are interdependent (i.e., no self-nature or existence on its own). Moreover, all phenomena and things are impermanent (changing constantly). It was to this law that Sakyamuni was awakened when he attained enlightenment.

Liberation: The state of complete freedom from suffering and its causes (ignorance/misperception of reality, selfish desire, attachment, and negative actions).

Lower Realms: The animal, hungry ghost, and hell realms, which are all part of cyclic existence or samsara.

Maha: Great.

Mahayana: lit. "great vehicle." A major branch of Buddhism practiced in China, Tibet, Japan, Korea, Vietnam, and Taiwan. The spiritual path to great enlightenment. The Mahayana goal is to attain Buddhahood for the benefit of all sentient beings by completely abandoning delusions and their imprints. The category created by a group of reformist sects of Indian Buddhism to distinguish themselves from the older preexisting sects. The Mahayana movement was characterized by a metaphysical theology which made extensive use of mythology and metaphorical supernatural events, the development of the Bodhisattva as a new model for the ideal practice of Buddhism, and a general impetus for the reformation of the monastic orders. The Mahayana is also noted for its advocacy of the laity and women as being capable of deep awakening, often depicting Bodhisattvas in the guise of lay people and women in scripture. The feminist aspect of this is particularly notable. It is probably the earliest example of a theological feminism in a major world religion.

Mala: A strand of prayer beads traditionally consisting of 108 beads. A mala is used for reciting a mantra or counting the breath during meditation practice.

Meditation: The process and practice of concentrating the mind and becoming deeply acquainted with one's own True Nature.

Metta: Loving-kindness.

Middle way: The practice of avoidance of extreme views and lifestyle choices.

(right) Mindfulness: The practice whereby a person is intentionally aware of his or her thoughts and actions in the present moment, non-judgmentally. The 7th step of the Noble Eightfold Path. One can practice mindfulness at all times, giving alert attention to all experiences without conceptualizing, judging, or controlling, allowing sensations, feelings, and thoughts to arise and disappear without being followed or resisted in any way. Such non-interfering attention allows one to be fully present in the experience of the moment. Mindfulness is also a state of awareness before the mind is disturbed by thought.

Namo: "Homage to." An exclamation showing reverence; devotion. Often placed in front of the name of an object of veneration, e.g., a Buddha's or Bodhisattva's name to express devotion to it. i.e. Namo Sakyamuni Buddha, Namo Amitaba, Namo Avalokitesvara.

Nirvana (Sanskrit) / **Nibbana** (Pali): The "unbinding" of the mind from passion, aversion, delusion. Awakening; liberation from the entire round of death and rebirth (samsara). The state of having extinguished suffering.

Nirvana is a spiritual state in which the bonds of existence are cut away. It is held to be an ineffable, indefinable experience. Nirvana/Nibanna also denotes the extinguishing of fire; it carries the connotations of stilling and cooling. Profound peace, limitless awareness, bliss, unity.

Om: The pure energy of the divine body of the Buddhas and Bodhisattvas.

Paramita (Sanskrit) / **Parami** (Pali): Perfection. Perfection of the character; perfect realization. To cross over to the other shore; reaching beyond limitation. The Paramitas are the framework of the Bodhisattva's religious practice, usually consisting of six categories, sometimes ten. These enlightened qualities or perfections are developed over many lifetimes by a Bodhisattva. The Six Paramitas are: Generosity/Charity (Dana), Virtue/Ethics (Sila), Patience/Forbearance (Kshanti), Effort/Perseverance (Virya), Concentration/Meditation (Dhyana), Wisdom (Pajna).

Parinirvana: Total unbinding; the complete cessation of the skandhas that occurs upon the death of an arhat/arahant. When the Buddha died, he did not die an ordinary death to be followed by rebirth. Because he had achieved complete enlightenment, his death is referred to as the parinirvana, because it was the end of all rebirths. This term also refers to the passing of any great realized person, in which they die and then can emanate back to aid sentient beings. However, their death and rebirth is propelled not by karma but by compassion.

Prajna (Sanskrit) / **Panna** (Pali): Wisdom: discernment; discriminative awareness; insight; intelligence. Understanding the nature of existence.

Preta (Sanskrit)/ **Peta** (Pali): A hungry ghost or famished spirit. One of a class of beings in the lower realms of samsara. Pretas are often depicted in Buddhist art as starving beings with tiny mouths through which they can never pass enough food to alleviate their hunger. The world of the pretas is characterized by the emotion of greed and the inability to appease their desires; a psychological characteristic of our own human nature.

Pure Lands: Realms beyond cyclic existence or samsara.

Rebirth: The process of continuity of life after death.

Refuge: Taking refuge involves the decision to integrate the Three Gems of Buddha, Dharma, and Sangha into one's life. Also see *Three Jewels*.

Samadhi: The mental state of being firmly fixed. The practice of fixing or centering the mind on a single sensation or object. Complete concentration; mental stability; a state of calm mental absorption from meditation practice.

Samsara: The cyclic cycle of death and rebirth. Samsara, characterized by dissatisfaction and suffering, is the cycle of death and rebirth in which all beings wander under the influence of karma. There are six realms of samsara. Listed in ascending order according to the type of karma that causes rebirth in them, they are the realms of the hell beings, hungry ghosts, animals, humans, demi-gods, and gods.

Samatha: Mental stabilization; tranquility meditation. Distinguished from vipassana meditation.

Sangha: Community of Buddhist practitioners. Those who are purely devoted to the virtuous path taught by Buddha. These are our best spiritual friends. In general, ordained or lay people who take Bodhisattva vows can be said to be sangha. More recently, the term 'sangha' has been popularly adapted to mean the wider sense of the 'community of followers on the Buddhist path.'

Sanskrit: The classical Aryan language of ancient India, systematized by scholars. With the exception of a few ancient translations probably from Pali versions, most of the original Buddhist texts used in China were Sanskrit.

Sentient Being: A being who has not yet reached enlightenment. The sentient being is generally defined as any living creature which has developed enough conscious awareness to experience feelings, particularly suffering. This generally includes all animal life and excludes botanical life forms. Sentient beings are the object of Buddhist ethics and compassion. Buddhism exists in a larger sense not simply to aid its own practitioners in their personal liberation, but also to function within the world to improve the conditions of life for all sentient beings.

Sakyamuni Buddha: "Sage of the Sakya clan."
Sakyamuni Buddha was the founder of Buddhism in this
age. He was born about 2600 years ago in what is now
Nepal as the Prince of the Sakyas and was called
Siddhartha Gautama. He attained supreme enlightenment
at age 35 and was called Sakyamuni. The word means
'capability and kindness.' Sakyamuni Buddha taught the
Dharma for the remaining years of his life. He died at the
age of 80 on the full moon night in May.

Siddhartha: The given name of Sakyamuni Buddha
when he was born to the King Suddhodana. The name
means "wish fulfilled."

Six Realms: See *Desire Realm*.

Sutra (Sanskrit) / Sutta (Pali): Literally, "thread." A
Buddhist scriptural text purporting to present a narrative
of a teaching given on a particular occasion by the
Buddha or sanctioned explicitly by the Buddha. The
sutras make up one section of the three sectioned canon
(Tripitaka). The other two are the monastic and ethical
code (Vinaya) and the body of canonized exegesis
(Abhidharma). A sutra/sutta is a discourse or sermon by
the Buddha or his contemporary disciples. After the
Buddha's death, the sutras/suttas were passed down in
the Pali language according to a well-established oral
tradition and were finally committed to written form in
Sri Lanka around 100 BCE. Over 10,000 sutras/suttas are
collected in the Sutta Pitaka, one of the principal bodies

of scriptural literature in Theravada Buddhism. The Pali
Suttas are widely regarded as the earliest record of the
Buddha's teachings.

Tathagata (Sanskrit and Pali): "One who has truly
gone" (tatha-gata) or "one who has become authentic"
(Tathagata). The living embodiment of Ultimate Reality.
An epithet used in ancient India for a person who has
attained the highest spiritual goal. In Buddhism, it
usually denotes the Buddha, although occasionally it can
also denote any of his arhat/arahant disciples.

Three Jewels: Also known as the "Three Precious Ones"
or the "Triple Gem," referring to the Buddha, the
Dharma, and the Sangha. The three essential components
of veneration and refuge in Buddhism. Buddhists take
refuge in the Three Jewels by pronouncing the threefold
refuge prayer, thus acknowledging themselves to be
Buddhists.

Three Marks of Existence: These are suffering
(dukkha), impermanence (anicca), and not-self or
egolessness (anatta). The direct experience and
realization of these through meditation is to see things as
they really are.

Vipashyana (Sanskrit) / Vipassana (Pali): Clear,
penetrating, and intuitive insight into physical and mental
phenomena as they arise and disappear, seeing them for
what they actually are, in and of themselves, free of
delusion. Vipashyana/Vipassana meditation develops
insight into the true nature of reality by gradually

dissolving one's egotistic sense of being a permanent self and reveals that consciousness is an open, dynamic field of spontaneously arising experiences. Insight (Vipashyana/Vipassana) meditation progresses through several stages, leading ultimately to the experience of pure dynamic emptiness or Nirvana. It is one of the two types of meditation found in all Buddhist traditions, the other being calm abiding or tranquility meditation (Samatha in Sanskrit).

Zen (Japanese): This school of Buddhism originally emerged from China and was known as Ch'an, a word derived from the Sanskrit word 'dhyana' which means meditation. The founder of Zen Buddhism was Bodhidharma, an Indian monk who came to China in 520 C.E. Zen passed from China to Japan in the thirteenth and fourteenth centuries. The Zen approach can be seen as quite radical, favoring meditation, intuition, and direct experience as a means to enlightenment rather than the scriptures. The transmission of the Zen lineage of teaching goes directly back to Sakyamuni Buddha and has been passed on, mind to mind, from teacher to disciple for the past 2600 years.

Smile and be well!

Author Bio

Quang Trí has been practicing meditation since 2002 and Buddhism since 2006. He is a Dharma teacher and a Truth seeker, teaching others about Buddhism and meditation. As the writer of the popular website, BuddhaJourney.net, Quang Trí continuously aspires to help everyone with their path toward Awakening through compassion, loving-kindness, appreciative joy and equanimity.